SOUTHERN
COOKING
GLOBAL
FLAVORS

SOUTHERN » COOKING GLOBAL « FLAVORS

RIZZOLI
NEW YORK

New York Paris London Milan

Foreword by
ALEXANDER SMALLS

Photography by
KRISTEN PENOYER

KENNY GILBERT and **Nan Kavanaugh**

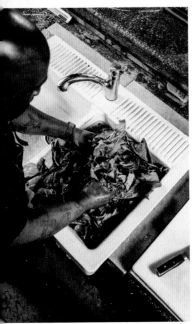

DEDICATION

To my mother and father, who nurtured a talent they saw in me and made our kitchen feel like a home.

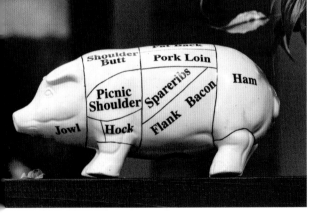

CONTENTS

Food . . . more than a notion . . . necessity. It's a revolution . . . a world of wonder . . . humble grace . . . ultimately a destination for the culinary enlightened, those among us who live and breathe the art of cooking and dining... serving up heaping helpings of love every day . . .

I have traveled the world in search of global flavors that mirror my cultural expression—a tasty woven tapestry of my own story, the story of my family, my community, and, ultimately, my ancestral trust on a storied plate...an edible discovery. During my travels through the foodways of the African diaspora, food has provided an interesting road map and a window into the legacy of "where we come from . . ." The intersection of the legacy cooking vessel and those recipe keepers charged with preserving the oral history of our culinary wealth for future generations provided comfort. Chefs and home cooks who will ultimately tell their stories, one dish at a time, continue the traditions of our shared humble beginnings, illuminating our shared culinary truth.

My curiosity about the world outside my reach and familiarity led me across rivers, lakes, mysterious oceans, lured by an unseen tribal force, to a people, customs, and traditions that spoke to the heart of my truth . . . despite the words of a foreign tongue. The common denominator was found in the ready pots that lined the tops of well-used stoves. The foods cooked proved that we were more alike than not . . . and spoke to me loudly. I was "kinfolk," I was home.

I saw myself, the boy in me, who dreamed I would find my tribe in a pot of my familiar . . . A kitchen table of recognizable grains and vegetables; a display of grains of rice, snap green beans, collard greens, black-eyed peas, and sweet potatoes mixed with oversized yams... If only a Negro Spiritual verse could deliver the bounty of my simple seduction, simplicity of my heritage, images bringing meaning to the fullness of life... The little boy in me who learned to stir his mama's pots, peel potatoes, and hoe rows of land in my grandpa's garden...held the seeds dropped from tiny hands, and who would one day understand the power of his deeds as a man. A man who would come to speak the language of culinary splendor and feed the world with his cheffing and culinary skills, who was driven by passion and curiosity, creating an edible conversation of love on a plate. A gumbo of freedom . . . joy . . . salvation on a platter of Southern fried chicken . . . This is what Southern cooking . . . African American foodways means to me . . . should mean to you . . . So take a seat at the table and let me fix a plate for you.

When I think of Chef Kenny Gilbert, I think of a man in search of ultimate flavor. I think of "good eating." I think of a master culinary practitioner who brings the full weight and force, and artistic expression, to the foods he interprets and invents, and then creates

and puts on a plate. Armed with the knowledge and collected grace of the ancestors, he continues to expand the narrative of our rich culinary inheritance. I think of an artisan at work, a man who brings his life and passion to every dish he conceives and creates . . . Chef Kenny is a seasoned veteran who has captured the heartbeat of the tradition of gathered ingredients, whether intended for a pot, casserole, sheet pan, or grill—even a skillet on the way to a waiting plate. He is a culinary warrior.

In his book *Southern Cooking · Global Flavors*, Chef Gilbert brings to life a newness to old-world goodness. An expression of ingredients, technical skills, and recipes for the modern kitchen, borrowing from different styles and flavors to put his own stamp on African American gastronomy. He is at home wherever there is fire. If he can create a flame he can cook anywhere and make anything table-worthy. His food speaks a language of love and engagement. Every dish tells a story, each bite is a memory recalled and savored. He was born to cook, set the table, and gift his unique culinary journey to all of us in this remarkable and colorful recipe-packed book. Amen!

INTRODUCTION

Cooking is a form of storytelling. A country's food culture tells the story of its people and their relationship with place. If you were to ask anyone in the world what constitutes American food, "burgers and fries" would most likely be the answer. Burgers and fries are American. My first job was in a McDonald's kitchen flipping burgers, and in America, you can find burgers and fries practically on every corner. But our food culture is so much more than fast food. We are a nation that is a melting pot, and the American home pantry tells our true story as a people.

Every American has their own food culture at home. Cooking at home is personal. I am a Black American descended from enslaved Africans. Staples of the American South like grits, collards, smoked ribs, fried fish, cornbread, baked mac & cheese, and fried chicken were regulars on our table at home when I was growing up. My dad was from Chicago and my mother was from St. Augustine, Florida. While our food culture at home was rooted in their shared heritage, there were also dishes specific to Cleveland, Ohio, where I grew up. For example, we ate fried chicken and spaghetti at home. Don't ask me why, but that's a common combination found in Cleveland; in Cincinnati, Ohio, they eat chili with their spaghetti.

Many Italians immigrated to Ohio in the early 1900s and brought with them their food culture. I remember going to a friend's house whose family heritage was Italian. Their refrigerator was full of capicola, salami, provolone, and all sorts of foods that were not in my home. As a kid, it was exciting to discover new foods this way, and my friends felt the same when eating at my house.

At home is where I learned about food and flavor. There, cooking was a part of everyday life. I used to hang out in the kitchen all the time while my mother cooked. My mother raised not one but two chefs. My brother also has a career in the culinary arts. It was important to our mother that we would be self-sufficient as men, which meant that we knew how to both cook and sew at a young age. I scrambled my first eggs at age three and made Thanksgiving dinner by age eleven. The only thing I can compare the experience to is kids who are put on skis or skateboards at an early age, and then you see them racing down a giant ramp. That's how cooking was for me. My mother let me start cooking at the stove at age three, and I took off from there.

As I grew older, cooking in restaurants was where I met Americans from all over the world who shared with me their food culture. A chef from Hawaii taught me about using meat spice-rub recipes that included coffee, which was common where he grew up on the Big Island. One of my best friends, Ray, is of Filipino heritage. He introduced me to

adobo while cooking the staff meal before service. Throughout my career cooking all over the United States, from Colorado to Miami, I have learned so much about the diversity of American food culture from the people I have worked with in restaurants.

This cookbook is a celebration of cultural influences that have coexisted in America over time. Throughout my career, I have had the opportunity to cook in kitchens in Asia, Europe, and the Caribbean. Here, I share my experience and expertise in understanding the authentic flavor profiles and cooking methods from across the world to create a cookbook that celebrates the multicultural American experience, grounded in my own personal food culture. It is my hope that this book will give you the confidence to cook authentic meals for friends of other ethnic backgrounds, use ingredients you may not be as familiar with, and spark interest in the variety of cultures that make up America.

This cookbook is easy to use. Each recipe contains a main dish and a side that are expertly paired based on flavor and texture. The ingredients for both are listed together for easy shopping, and all can be found in local grocery stores and ethnic markets. I encourage you to explore the various ethnic markets in your area when shopping. They are wonderful places to learn about the different cultures of America, and you will find new foods to enjoy. If you do not have ethnic markets where you live, specialty ingredients can also be found online. This is one of the great bonuses of a globalized world.

Cooking is an act of sharing, and it is in that place of generosity that we are the most humane. There is a place in American culture for the thirty-minute meal, but there is also a place for the three-hour dinner. If there is one thing we can all learn from cooking an epic meal, it is that it is okay to slow down. The recipes presented here take time to prepare. A kitchen is a place of learning, and learning takes time.

This cookbook allows readers to expand their own kitchen culture. It provides the opportunity to treat cooking not as a chore, but as an experience to be shared with family and friends. Stories are told in kitchens over cooking as much as they are told through cooking. Our pantries all have their own stories to tell, and we all have a lot to learn from sharing them.

Food is one of the great common denominators of humanity. A delicious meal brings people together unlike any other experience. I love food. To learn the global cuisines presented in this cookbook, I have researched and studied, traveled and trained. I hope that sharing my journey and knowledge in this book will empower readers to be open to new foods and maybe, just maybe, to new people too. This is an exploration of American food culture with the mindset that we are all human, and we all bring different things to the table that are to be respected, shared, and honored.

KITCHEN PANTRY

Throughout this cookbook, you might find ingredients that are unfamiliar. This guide is designed to help navigate where to shop for these goods and to offer a better understanding of how they serve each recipe.

Agave nectar
WHERE TO FIND: grocery store/online
NOTES: Sweetener made from several species of agave. A great sweetener substitute that I like to use in Latin-inspired dishes.

Artichoke hearts (baby, canned or fresh)
WHERE TO FIND: gourmet grocery stores
NOTES: Baby artichokes are less fussy than the adult plant. Remove a few leaves and the entire vegetable is ready to eat. These can be bought fresh, canned or brined, or marinated in olive oil and herbs. I think Sid Wainer & Son has the best brined and marinated versions on the market.

Asiago cheese
WHERE TO FIND: grocery store
NOTES: Cow's-milk cheese from Italy. The cheese can have different textures based on age. I like the sharp and creamy flavor.

Asian pears
WHERE TO FIND: Asian markets
NOTES: Native fruit of East Asia. Used in Korean cuisine in marinades for meats. The enzymes in the fruit act as a natural tenderizer.

Baby bok choy
WHERE TO FIND: Asian markets
NOTES: Also known as Chinese cabbage. I love the flavor of this cabbage and like to use it in Asian-inspired dishes.

Baby corn
WHERE TO FIND: Asian markets
NOTES: Baby corn is a young ear of corn that can be eaten whole. A great alternative to shucked corn for presentations and flavor variations.

Bamboo rice
WHERE TO FIND: Asian markets
NOTES: Short-grain rice colored and flavored by bamboo juice. Great for starchy rice dishes like risotto or congee.

Benne seeds
WHERE TO FIND: online
NOTES: Strain of sesame seed from Africa. Available from Anson Mills Farm in South Carolina.

Bird or Thai chiles
WHERE TO FIND: Asian markets
NOTES: Also known as bird's-eye chiles; they are quite hot, measuring 50,000–100,000 on the Scoville scale.

Black truffle oil
WHERE TO FIND: online
NOTES: Extra-virgin olive oil infused with black truffles.

Bouillon (chicken, beef, and shrimp)
WHERE TO FIND: grocery store, online, Asian markets
NOTES: Bouillon is stock that has been dehydrated.

Boursin cheese (garlic and herb)
WHERE TO FIND: grocery stores
NOTES: Soft, creamy cow's-milk cheese infused with garlic and fines herbes.

Branzino
WHERE TO FIND: fish markets
NOTES: European sea bass

Calamansi juice
WHERE TO FIND: online
NOTES: Citrus juice from the Philippines. Very tart flavor similar to combining lime, lemon, and orange juices.

Cane syrup
WHERE TO FIND: online
NOTES: Sugarcane juice that has been cooked down to a syrup. My favorite brand is Alaga.

Cassareep
WHERE TO FIND: Caribbean markets; online
NOTES: Cassareep is the extract of cassava root infused with different hard spices. This is a key

ingredient for Guyanese pepperpot. You could substitute with a touch of molasses combined with cayenne pepper, clove, cinnamon, and salt.

Chef Kenny Gilbert spices

WHERE TO FIND: online
NOTES: Raging Cajun, Cinnamon Coffee Rub, Fried Chicken Seasoning, Moroccan Spice, and Jerk Spice. A set of low-sodium spice mixes that will wake up the flavor of any dish. (To make about ½ cup **cinnamon coffee rub**: 4 tablespoons instant coffee granules, 4 teaspoons Cajun seasoning, 4 teaspoons cumin, 4 teaspoons cinnamon, 4 teaspoons coriander. Store in a spice jar.)

Chipotles in adobo sauce

WHERE TO FIND: grocery store; Mexican markets
NOTES: Smoked and dried jalapeño peppers simmered in a tomato sauce with additional spices such as cumin and coriander.

Cotija cheese

WHERE TO FIND: grocery stores; Mexican markets
NOTES: Aged cow's milk-cheese that is crumbly. Its named after the town of Cotija, Michoacán.

Creole mustard

WHERE TO FIND: grocery stores, online
NOTES: Stone-ground mustard pureed with vinegar. It has a coarse texture and spicy flavor.

Duck fat

WHERE TO FIND: gourmet grocery stores; online
NOTES: Rendered fat from ducks.

Espelette pepper

WHERE TO FIND: online
NOTES: A ground red chile pepper from France. It has a subtle heat with a slight sea brine and hints of peach.

Fennel pollen

WHERE TO FIND: online
NOTES: Also called "culinary fairy dust." The pollen is harvested from the dried flowers of the fennel plant. Great on seafood and with pasta and pork dishes.

Fish sauce

WHERE TO FIND: Asian markets; grocery stores; online
NOTES: Fish sauce is made from anchovy extract, water, salt, fructose, and hydrolyzed wheat protein. My favorite brand is Three Crabs.

Fried garlic

WHERE TO FIND: Asian markets; online
NOTES: Garlic that has been either chopped or sliced, then fried. Super convenient product.

Fried shallots

WHERE TO FIND: Asian markets; online
NOTES: Shallots that are sliced thin and fried until crispy.

Ginseng root extract/tea granules

WHERE TO FIND: Asian markets
NOTES: Korean ginseng root has been used for centuries as a tonic to help treat patients with chronic illnesses. The flavor is very distinct and works well in braised dishes and soups.

Golden Mountain Boy seasoning sauce

WHERE TO FIND: Asian markets; online
NOTES: A Thai seasoning sauce that some consider a "secret sauce." Some prefer to use it instead of fish sauce in dishes. It does contain soy.

Grapeseed oil
WHERE TO FIND: grocery stores; online
NOTES: Oil extracted from grapes.

Green papaya
WHERE TO FIND: Asian markets
NOTES: Unripened papaya, classically used in Thai salads or slaws.

Ground green or black cardamom
WHERE TO FIND: gourmet grocery stores; online
NOTES: Spice from India used widely in Indian dishes.

Ground sumac
WHERE TO FIND: Middle Eastern markets; online
NOTES: The ground dried berries of a flowering plant, sumac has a lemony or sour flavor. It is very popular in Mediterranean dishes and is used in spice rubs, marinades, and dressings.

Ground turmeric
WHERE TO FIND: Middle Eastern markets; online
NOTES: Turmeric is a root very popular in Indian cuisine. It has many proven health benefits. It is one of the main components in Madras curry powder and is a yellow color.

Guava paste
WHERE TO FIND: Caribbean markets; online
NOTES: Guava is a fruit grown in Latin America and the Caribbean. The fruit is naturally sweet when ripe and has a slight tartness. The fruit is cooked down and made into a paste. It is served in many dishes.

Kimchi base
WHERE TO FIND: Asian markets; online
NOTES: Kimchi base consists of pickled cabbage pieces and red chiles. This base can be added to cabbage to make your own kimchi or added to sauces, broths, and/or marinades to bring flavors from Korea into your meal. I prefer Momoya or Kimuchi No Moto brands.

Kombu
WHERE TO FIND: Asian markets; online
NOTES: Kombu is edible dried kelp. It provides umami flavor to dishes. It's great in broths or

salads and delicious fried as a snack seasoned with salt, pepper, sugar, and sesame seeds.

Korean rice cakes
WHERE TO FIND: Asian markets; online
NOTES: Korean rice cakes are made from a combination of rice and tapioca starch. The tapioca starch gives this dumpling a chewy texture.

Kosher salt
WHERE TO FIND: grocery stores
NOTES: Kosher salt is a coarse salt without common additives such as iodine.

Lard
WHERE TO FIND: grocery stores
NOTES: Lard is rendered pig fat. Commonly used in the past for baking, frying, charcuterie, and preserving.

Lemongrass (powder and paste)
WHERE TO FIND: Asian markets; online
NOTES: Lemongrass or "barbed wire" grass has a very fragrant lemony aroma and flavor. Also called citronella grass, it is used in Asian, African, and Australian cuisines.

Limoncello
WHERE TO FIND: liquor stores; online
NOTES: Limoncello is an Italian lemon liqueur.

Liquid smoke
WHERE TO FIND: grocery stores; online
NOTES: Liquid smoke is used as a flavoring in place of the smoky flavor you'd get from cooking over a wood fire.

Madras curry powder
WHERE TO FIND: South Asian markets; online
NOTES: Madras curry powder is a spicier version of regular curry powder. The spice comes from chile peppers that are added to the blend.

Makrut lime leaves or powder
WHERE TO FIND: Asian markets
NOTES: Makrut lime is a citrus fruit native to Southeast Asia. The leaves can be found fresh or dried and ground into a powder. It has a very distinctive flavor that is popular in Southeast Asian dishes.

Marsala

WHERE TO FIND: grocery or liquor stores

NOTES: A fortified dry or sweet wine produced in the city of Marsala in Sicily. It's beautiful to cook with and especially pairs well with mushrooms.

Mascarpone cheese

WHERE TO FIND: gourmet grocery stores

NOTES: Mascarpone cheese is a soft, acidic Italian cream cheese. BelGioioso is a brand commonly found in grocery stores and markets.

Miso paste

WHERE TO FIND: Asian markets; online

NOTES: Miso paste is a traditional Japanese seasoning of fermented soybean paste, salt, and koji, rice cultured with an edible fungus.

Panang curry paste

WHERE TO FIND: Middle Eastern markets; online

NOTES: Panang curry paste is a milder version of red curry paste. The color is a bit softer since it contains less tomato paste and red peppers. It usually also contains ground peanuts. It is often usued in seafood dishes.

Pancetta

WHERE TO FIND: grocery stores

NOTES: Pancetta is an Italian un-smoked pork belly salume. It is often used for flavoring soups and pastas.

Panko breadcrumbs

WHERE TO FIND: grocery stores

NOTES: Panko breadcrumbs are a Japanese-style dried bread crumb with a distinctive coarse texture.

Pepitas

WHERE TO FIND: grocery stores; Mexican markets

NOTES: Pepitas are hulled pumpkin seeds. They can be purchased raw or roasted.

Pernod

WHERE TO FIND: liquor stores; online

NOTES: Pernod is a pungent, strong, licorice-flavored liqueur.

Porcini mushrooms (dried and powdered)

WHERE TO FIND: online

NOTES: Porcini mushrooms are an Italian mushroom that have a very fragrant flavor. They can be found more commonly dried or in powder form.

Potato starch

WHERE TO FIND: gourmet grocery stores; online

NOTES: Potato starch is a cornstarch substitute made from dehydrated potatoes. It has more nutrients than cornstarch.

Rapini, broccoli rabe

WHERE TO FIND: gourmet and other grocery stores

NOTES: Rapini, or broccoli rabe, is a green vegetable related to the turnip. It has a slightly bitter flavor.

Red quinoa

WHERE TO FIND: health food stores; online

NOTES: Quinoa is an ancient grain (technically a seed) from South America. It has a great nutty flavor.

Rice flour

WHERE TO FIND: gourmet grocery stores

NOTES: Rice flour is flour made from ground rice.

Saffron

WHERE TO FIND: Middle Eastern markets; online

NOTES: Saffron is harvested from a type of crocus. You can get it in thread or powder form; I use the thread form.

Saint André cheese

WHERE TO FIND: gourmet grocery stores

NOTES: A triple-cream cow's-milk cheese from France with a powdery white rind.

San Marzano tomatoes

WHERE TO FIND: grocery stores

NOTES: San Marzano tomatoes are a type of Roma tomato from the areas between Naples and Salerno, Italy.

Scottish salmon

WHERE TO FIND: fish markets

NOTES: Scottish Salmon is considered to be the best in the world. It has a mild, buttery flavor and higher fat content compared to other species of salmon.

Self-Rising Flour
WHERE TO FIND: grocery stores
NOTES: Self-rising flour has a raising agent, like baking powder, and salt already incorporated. My favorite brand is White Lily. It makes for a softer, fluffier biscuit.

Sesame oil
WHERE TO FIND: grocery stores; Asian markets; online
NOTES: Sesame oil is oil made from pressed sesame seeds.

Shrimp paste
WHERE TO FIND: Asian markets; online
NOTES: There are many versions of shrimp paste. I prefer the shrimp paste in soybean oil. Pantai is my favorite brand.

Sweet plantains
WHERE TO FIND: grocery stores
NOTES: Sweet plantains can be pre-ripened and frozen in a number of forms. The most common are sliced pieces.

Taleggio
WHERE TO FIND: gourmet grocery stores
NOTES: Taleggio is a cow's-milk cheese with a washed rind, from Italy. It has a strong nutty flavor.

Tasso ham
WHERE TO FIND: gourmet grocery stores; meat markets
NOTES: Tasso ham is a cured smoked pork shoulder commonly used in Creole cuisine.

Tempura flour
WHERE TO FIND: Asian markets; grocery stores; online
NOTES: Tempura flour is used specifically for making tempura batter for fried items. It is made of many flours, and is easier to buy than to make.

Thai basil
WHERE TO FIND: Asian markets
NOTES: Thai basil is a specific type of basil commonly used in Thai cuisine.

Vanilla (extract, beans, and paste)
WHERE TO FIND: grocery stores; online
NOTES: Vanilla is a flavoring derived from orchids. It can come in many forms, including whole bean, paste, extract, and powder.

White truffle oil
WHERE TO FIND: gourmet grocery stores; online
NOTES: Olive oil infused with truffles. It is used to add truffle flavor to dishes.

Xanthan gum
WHERE TO FIND: grocery stores; online
NOTES: Xanthan gum is a powdered food additive widely used as an emulsifier and stabilizer, which helps to keep foods from separating.

Wasabi paste
WHERE TO FIND: gourmet grocery stores; Asian markets
NOTES: Japanese horseradish traditionally used with sushi.

FRIED CHICKEN + BISCUITS

THE FLAVOR BOMB

Smoky fried chicken thighs tossed in Flavor Bomb Sauce on a
black truffle–smoked Gouda biscuit with chives

26

THE FLORIDA-GEORGIA BOY

Southern fried chicken breasts topped with cane syrup butter
on a buttermilk drop biscuit

32

THE KOREAN

Crispy Korean fried chicken breasts tossed in
gochujang honey sauce, topped with toasted benne seeds and
sandwiched in a plantain-ginger biscuit with turmeric

36

KUNG PAO

Fried chicken thighs tossed in kung pao sauce
topped with pickled-ginger slaw and sandwiched
in a decadent peanut butter biscuit

40

CHICKEN PARMESAN

Chicken cutlets breaded and fried in Italian-style crumbs
topped with marinara sauce, fresh mozzarella cheese,
and basil on an Asiago-garlic biscuit

46

Chicken and biscuits: a combination that reminds me of the comfort of home more than any other dish in my bag. Fried chicken dinner was a staple weeknight meal in my house when I was growing up. I learned to make fried chicken from my mom. She would scrub the kitchen sink, then place raw chicken in the basin and rinse it off. Still in the sink, she would season the meat with Lawry's seasoning salt, granulated garlic, lemon pepper, and black pepper. She'd melt Crisco in a hot cast-iron skillet. While it heated up, Mom would flour the chicken, tossing it until it was tacky. She would flick a little flour into the skillet to see if the grease was crackling hot. Then she dusted the chicken with a dry coat of flour. Mom would wait for me to arrive home from school, and as soon as I walked in the door, she'd drop the chicken in the oil to fry. By the time I had showered and dressed for dinner, it was ready. Mom's fried chicken always came out crispy brown. I ate it with Texas Pete hot sauce or Tabasco, and it'd make my nose burn. I have always liked my fried chicken either cold or screamin' hot.

A pile of warm biscuits was a regular side at the table as well. I would doctor up the store-bought dough my mom kept in the fridge with sugar or syrup before they went into the oven. I began to bake my own biscuits when I was eleven years old using a recipe from *The Betty Crocker Cookbook*. It called for rolling out the dough, which certainly required a little more energy than just popping open a tube, pulling apart the biscuits, and sticking them in the oven. But I found making biscuits from scratch much more rewarding. I have since learned there are many ways to make a biscuit, and drop biscuits are my favorite. A drop biscuit is a quick bread that is easy and delicious. Instead of rolling out the dough and layering it, a drop biscuit is mixed or kneaded, then scooped and dropped onto a lined sheet pan. Since no rolling is required, it is easier to adapt a drop biscuit with different ingredients like plantains or cheeses. When baking, their aroma fills the kitchen, which always fills me with nostalgia, reminding me of time spent with my mom.

In the South, fried chicken and biscuits is a dish that speaks to family time. It is served at large gatherings and simple weeknight dinners. A single chicken can feed a family of four, and with a stack of biscuits, you have an inexpensive, mouthwatering meal. I feel that fried chicken and biscuits are loved by just about everyone and can be easily adapted to incorporate the flavors of many cultures, which is what I've done here. Fried chicken is crispy. It's hot. It's juicy. The smell of it crackling on the stove is love. Combined with warm biscuits and your choice of condiments, you have a dish that reminds us all that some foods just feel like home.

The Flavor Bomb

Over the years I have tailored my fried chicken recipe to the palate of Ms. Oprah Winfrey. My good friend, Chef Sonny Sweetman, introduced me to Ms. Winfrey in 2014, and I have been one of her personal chefs ever since. One Saturday at her home, Woody Harrelson, Willie Nelson, and their wives came for dinner. It was a beautiful Maui evening, and dinner was being prepared outside. I was standing at the buffet when Ms. Winfrey came walking up. As we were speaking, Gayle King's son, Will, returned for seconds. He had made his biscuit sandwich with both my Fernandina Beach hot sauce and local honey—the combination that inspired my Flavor Bomb Sauce. Will suggested she try it and Ms. Winfrey took his advice. Later she said, "Kenny, it is worth flying you out here just for your fried chicken and biscuits."

INGREDIENTS

SERVES 6

FOR THE BRINE
6 (5-ounce) boneless, skinless chicken thighs
1 cup water
1 cup buttermilk
Juice of 2 lemons (¼ cup)
3 tablespoons low-sodium soy sauce
2 tablespoons liquid smoke
2 tablespoons Chef Kenny's Fried Chicken Seasoning, or other poultry seasoning
2 tablespoons Chef Kenny's Raging Cajun Spice, or other Cajun seasoning
1 tablespoon kosher salt

FOR THE FLAVOR BOMB SAUCE
Makes 4 cups

1 cup vegetable shortening
1 cup honey
1 cup water
½ cup apple cider vinegar
½ cup jarred roasted red peppers with juice
¼ cup Creole mustard
3 fresh habanero peppers
5 cloves garlic, peeled
2 navel oranges, cut into quarters
1 small Spanish onion, sliced (½ cup)
2 tablespoons kosher salt
1 tablespoon Chef Kenny's Raging Cajun Spice, or other Cajun seasoning
1 tablespoon Chef Kenny's Fried Chicken Seasoning, or other poultry seasoning

2 teaspoons crushed red pepper
1 teaspoon freshly ground black pepper
¼ teaspoon xanthan gum

FOR THE BISCUITS
4 cups self-rising flour, plus more for dusting
1 cup buttermilk
½ cup granulated sugar
4 tablespoons (½ stick) salted butter, melted
¼ cup vegetable shortening
¼ cup dried chives
8 ounces smoked Gouda cheese, grated (1 cup)
2 large eggs
2 tablespoons black truffle oil
1 tablespoon apple cider vinegar
1 tablespoon Chef Kenny's Fried Chicken Seasoning, or other poultry seasoning
1 tablespoon kosher salt
1 teaspoon xanthan gum

FOR THE DREDGE AND FRY
4 cups canola or corn oil
1 pound lard
1 cup self-rising flour
½ cup cornstarch
½ cup rice flour
¼ cup Chef Kenny's Fried Chicken Seasoning, or other poultry seasoning
2 large eggs

Brine the Chicken

1. Place the chicken thighs into a 1-gallon resealable plastic bag.
2. In a medium bowl, whisk the water, buttermilk, lemon juice, soy sauce, liquid smoke, chicken and Cajun seasonings, and salt.
3. Pour the brine into the plastic bag with the chicken thighs and toss with your hands to thoroughly coat the chicken.
4. Seal the bag and place in the refrigerator. Brine for a minimum of 15 minutes and up to 24 hours.

Make the Flavor Bomb Sauce

1. In a medium saucepan, combine the shortening, honey, water, vinegar, roasted red peppers, mustard, habaneros, garlic, oranges, onion, salt, Cajun and chicken seasonings, crushed red pepper, black pepper, and xanthan gum. Cook over medium heat, stirring occasionally, for 30 minutes.
2. Check a habanero pepper and an orange wedge for doneness. If they can be pierced easily with a knife, they are soft enough. Puree the mixture with a handheld stick blender until smooth. Set aside at room temperature. (This sauce can be stored in an airtight container in the refrigerator for up to 3 months. Leftovers are a great sweet and spicy condiment that can be used for chicken wings, pork chops, ribs, fried cauliflower, and much more.)

Make the Biscuits

1. In a large bowl, mix the flour, buttermilk, sugar, melted butter, shortening, dried chives, Gouda, eggs, truffle oil, apple cider vinegar, chicken seasoning, salt, and xanthan gum by hand, just until the dough starts to come together. Alternatively, you can mix the ingredients in the bowl of a stand mixer with the dough hook. Mix on low speed for 2 minutes, just until the dough starts to come together.
2. Line a sheet pan with parchment paper. Using an ice cream scoop, portion out 6 large biscuits. Lightly dust each biscuit with flour and lightly press them down with a spatula or small bowl to a ½-inch thickness.
3. Transfer the sheet pan to the refrigerator and chill the biscuits for at least 15 minutes, or until firm to the touch. Preheat the oven to 375°F.
4. Bake for 15 minutes on the middle rack of the oven. Rotate the sheet pan and bake for another 8 minutes, until the biscuit tops are golden brown. Remove and allow to cool to room temperature. Reduce the oven temperature to 170°F.

Make the Dredge and Fry the Chicken

1. Heat a 14- or 16-inch cast-iron skillet or frying pan on medium-low. Put the oil and lard in the skillet and heat for 20 minutes.
2. Mix the self-rising flour, cornstarch, rice flour, and chicken seasoning in a large bowl.
3. Remove the bag of brined chicken from the fridge. Whisk the eggs in a small bowl. Add the eggs to the bag, seal, and thoroughly coat the chicken with the egg by massaging the bag.

4. Working with one piece of chicken at a time, dredge each piece in the flour mixture, then set on a plate. Let the chicken rest for 3 to 5 minutes; reserve the flour mixture.

5. Check the temperature of the oil in the skillet with an instant-read thermometer. Once it reaches 325° to 350°F, dredge the chicken again in the flour mixture. (Note: The first dredging of the chicken creates the first layer of batter on the chicken, while the second dredge adds the crunch factor.)

6. Gently set half the chicken pieces in the hot oil and fry for 2 minutes. Turn each piece with a long-handled strainer or spider and fry for another 5 to 7 minutes, until golden brown and crispy.

7. Transfer the chicken to a plate lined with paper towels. Check the temperature of the chicken. If the chicken is under 165°F, return it to the skillet and continue to cook, flipping the chicken often to ensure even cooking. Move the cooked batch to a sheet pan and place in the warm oven. Continue until all the chicken is fried. Remove the chicken from the oven to briefly toast the biscuits. Increase the oven temperature to 400°F.

The Build

1. Halve the biscuits and place on a parchment paper–lined sheet pan. Toast in the oven for 5 minutes.

2. Place the fried chicken in a large bowl and gently toss with 3 cups of the Flavor Bomb Sauce until well coated.

3. Top the bottom half of each biscuit with a piece of fried chicken, followed by the biscuit lid. Plate the remaining servings and serve any remaining sauce alongside.

The Florida-Georgia Boy

Cooking and sharing a meal can often help us to make the best of difficult times. This recipe was born during the Covid-19 pandemic shutdown, the toughest time for the restaurant industry. My good friend Chef Scotty Schwartz landed a catering gig cooking breakfast and lunch for a hundred nurses and first responders at testing sites throughout northeast Florida. He invited me to team up with him and his staff to provide meals for these heroes. The hours were hard. The breakfast shift started at 3:00 a.m. In the early hours, it was just the two of us in the kitchen. We were in our element—prepping, cooking, and talking about food and life. At some point we'd make breakfast for ourselves. One morning chicken and biscuits were on the menu, and Scotty made a honey butter for the biscuit sandwiches that was amazing.

Scotty, a Jewish "Georgia boy" from Atlanta, is both a friend and a business associate. We met over a decade ago, early in our restaurateur careers on Amelia Island and have a strong mutual respect. Both our culinary roots are in Southern food, but from different cultures. He grew up eating honey on biscuits, while I grew up eating Alaga cane syrup on everything. Alaga has a rich and decadent sweetness, but is not as sweet as honey nor as bitter or rich as molasses. Sugarcane is a big crop in Florida, which is where my grandmother lived. This recipe celebrates our Southern upbringings, our friendship, and how there is always something to learn when friends cook together in the kitchen.

INGREDIENTS

SERVES 6

FOR THE BRINE
6 (5-ounce) boneless, skinless chicken breasts
1 cup water
1 cup buttermilk
Juice of 2 lemons (¼ cup)
2 tablespoons low-sodium soy sauce
1 tablespoon kosher salt
1 tablespoon Chef Kenny's Fried Chicken
   Seasoning, or other poultry seasoning
1 tablespoon Chef Kenny's Raging Cajun Spice,
   or other Cajun seasoning

FOR THE CANE SYRUP BUTTER
Makes 1½ cups
1 cup (2 sticks) salted butter, softened
½ cup pure cane syrup

FOR THE BISCUITS
4 cups self-rising flour, plus more for dusting
1 cup buttermilk
½ cup granulated sugar
4 tablespoons (½ stick) salted butter, melted
¼ cup vegetable shortening
2 large eggs
1 tablespoon apple cider vinegar
1 tablespoon kosher salt
1 teaspoon xanthan gum

FOR THE DREDGE AND FRY
4 cups canola or corn oil
1 pound lard
1 cup self-rising flour
½ cup cornstarch
½ cup rice flour
¼ cup Chef Kenny's Fried Chicken Seasoning,
   or other poultry seasoning
2 large eggs

Brine the Chicken	**1.** Cover the surface of a large cutting board with plastic wrap and place the chicken breasts on top. Lay another piece of plastic wrap flat over the chicken, sandwiching the breasts between the two pieces. Using a mallet, pound the chicken breasts until they are about ¼ inch thick.
	2. Place the chicken breasts into a 1-gallon resealable plastic bag.
	3. In a medium bowl, whisk the water, buttermilk, lemon juice, soy sauce, salt, chicken seasoning, and Cajun seasoning.
	4. Pour the brine into the plastic bag with the chicken breasts and toss with your hands to thoroughly coat the chicken.
	5. Seal the bag and place in the refrigerator. Brine for a minimum of 15 minutes and up to 24 hours.

Make the Cane Syrup Butter	**1.** Place the butter and cane syrup in the bowl of a stand mixer with the paddle attachment.
	2. Mix on low speed for 3 to 4 minutes, until the cane syrup and butter are fully incorporated.
	3. Transfer to an airtight container with a lid. (This butter can be made days in advance. Stored in the refrigerator, it is good for up to 30 days. Use any leftovers as an alternative to regular butter on toast, pancakes, or French toast.)

Make the Biscuits	**1.** Preheat the oven to 375°F.
	2. In a large bowl, mix the flour, buttermilk, sugar, melted butter, shortening, eggs, apple cider vinegar, salt, and xanthan gum by hand, just until the dough starts to come together. Alternatively, you can mix the ingredients in the bowl of a stand mixer with the dough hook. Mix on low speed for 1 minute. Scrape the bowl with a rubber spatula and then mix for another minute, just until the dough starts to come together.
	3. Line a sheet pan with parchment paper. Using an ice cream scoop, portion out 6 large biscuits. Lightly dust each biscuit with flour and lightly press them down with a spatula or small bowl to a ½-inch thickness.
	4. Transfer the sheet pan to the refrigerator and chill the biscuits for at least 15 minutes, or until firm to the touch. Preheat the oven to 375°F.
	5. Bake for 15 minutes on the middle rack of the oven. Rotate the sheet pan and bake for another 8 minutes, until the biscuit tops are golden brown. Remove and allow to cool to room temperature. Reduce the oven temperature to 170°F.

Make the Dredge and Fry the Chicken	**1.** Heat a 14- or 16-inch cast-iron skillet or frying pan on medium-low. Put the oil and lard in the skillet and heat for 20 minutes.
	2. Mix the self-rising flour, cornstarch, rice flour, and chicken seasoning in a large bowl.
	3. Remove the bag of brined chicken from the fridge. Whisk the eggs in a small bowl. Add the eggs to the bag, seal, and thoroughly coat the chicken with the egg by massaging the bag.

4. Working with one piece of chicken at a time, dredge each piece in the flour mixture, then set on a plate. Let the chicken rest for 3 to 5 minutes; reserve the flour mixture.
5. Check the temperature of the oil in the skillet with an instant-read thermometer. Once it reaches 325° to 350°F, dredge the chicken again in the flour mixture. (Note: The first dredging of the chicken creates the first layer of batter on the chicken, while the second dredge adds the crunch factor.)
6. Gently set half the chicken pieces in the hot oil and fry for 2 minutes. Turn each piece with a long-handled strainer or spider and fry for another 5 to 7 minutes, until golden brown and crispy.
7. Transfer the chicken to a plate lined with paper towels. Check the temperature of the chicken. If the chicken is under 165°F, return it to the skillet and continue to cook, flipping the chicken often to ensure even cooking. Move the cooked batch to a sheet pan and place in the warm oven. Continue until all the chicken is fried. Remove the chicken from the oven to briefly toast the biscuits. Increase the oven temperature to 400°F.

The Build

1. Halve the biscuits and place on a parchment paper–lined sheet pan. Toast in the oven for 5 minutes.
2. Place the bottom half of a biscuit on a plate and top with a fried chicken breast. Add a small scoop (about 1½ ounces) of cane syrup butter on top of the chicken breast, followed by the biscuit lid. Plate the remaining servings.

The Korean

When I was the chef at the Ritz-Carlton on Amelia Island, off Florida's Atlantic coast, we used to have staff family meals on Saturdays. I worked with a Korean man named Chulhun Jeon. He introduced me to a lot of Korean food, and it got me interested. I started going to Korean restaurants and found one of my all-time favorite restaurants, Sam Won Garden, in Jacksonville, Florida. One of the things I loved, as a part of the Korean BBQ there, was getting a little dish of gochujang (Korean fermented chile and bean paste) and another with sesame oil with salt and pepper in it. I would take both and mix them together with a little soy, then dip my barbecue in it. It was so delicious. In this recipe I wanted to emulate classic Korean fried chicken and include the flavors of that amazing sweet, tangy, and slightly spicy sauce.

INGREDIENTS

SERVES 6

FOR THE BRINE
6 (5-ounce) boneless, skinless chicken breasts
1 cup water
1 cup buttermilk
¼ cup apple cider vinegar
2 tablespoons low-sodium soy sauce
¼ cup ground ginger
1 tablespoon kosher salt

FOR THE GOCHUJANG HONEY
Makes 2 cups

1 cup honey
1 cup gochujang paste

FOR THE BISCUITS
5 cups self-rising flour, plus more for dusting
2 cups frozen, thawed sweet plantains
½ cup granulated sugar
¼ cup ground ginger
2 tablespoons ground turmeric
1 tablespoon kosher salt
1 teaspoon xanthan gum
1 cup buttermilk
4 tablespoons (½ stick) salted butter, melted
¼ cup vegetable shortening
2 large eggs
1 tablespoon apple cider vinegar

FOR THE DREDGE AND FRY
8 cups canola or corn oil
1 cup self-rising flour
½ cup cornstarch
½ cup rice flour
¼ cup ground ginger
2 large eggs

FOR THE BUILD
2 tablespoons benne or sesame seeds

Brine the Chicken

1. Cover the surface of a large cutting board with plastic wrap and place the chicken breasts on top. Lay another piece of plastic wrap flat over the chicken, sandwiching the breasts between the two pieces. Using a mallet, pound the chicken breasts until they are about ¼ inch thick.
2. Place the chicken breasts inside a 1-gallon resealable plastic bag.
3. In a medium bowl, whisk the water, buttermilk, apple cider vinegar, soy sauce, ground ginger, and salt.
4. Pour the brine into the plastic bag with the chicken breasts and toss with your hands to thoroughly coat the chicken.
5. Seal the bag and place in the refrigerator. Brine for a minimum of 15 minutes and up to 24 hours.

Make the Gochujang Honey

Whisk the honey and gochujang in a small mixing bowl until well incorporated. Cover and reserve. (The sauce can be made in advance. Stored in an airtight container in the refrigerator, it will be keep for 6 months. Any leftovers can be used as a dipping sauce for fried vegetables, seafood, poultry, and pork.)

Make the Biscuits

1. Place the flour, sweet plantains, sugar, ginger, turmeric, salt, and xanthan gum in the bowl of a stand mixer with the dough hook. Mix on low speed for 2 minutes.
2. When the mixture looks like wet sand, stop and scrape the sides of the bowl with a rubber spatula.
3. Add the buttermilk, melted butter, shortening, eggs, and apple cider vinegar and continue mixing on low for another 2 minutes, until the dough comes together into a ball.
4. Line a sheet pan with parchment paper. Using an ice cream scoop, portion out 6 large biscuits. Lightly dust each biscuit with flour and lightly press them down with a spatula or small bowl to a ½-inch thickness.
5. Transfer the sheet pan to the refrigerator and chill the biscuits for at least 15 minutes, or until firm to the touch. Preheat the oven to 375°F.
6. Bake for 15 minutes on the middle rack of the oven. Rotate the sheet pan and bake for another 8 minutes, until the biscuit tops are golden brown. Remove and allow to cool to room temperature. Reduce the oven temperature to 170°F.

Make the Dredge and Fry the Chicken

1. Heat a 14- or 16-inch cast-iron skillet or frying pan on medium-low. Put the oil in the skillet and heat for 20 minutes.
2. Mix the self-rising flour, cornstarch, rice flour, and ginger in a large bowl.
3. Remove the bag of brined chicken from the fridge. Whisk the eggs in a small bowl. Add the eggs to the bag, seal, and thoroughly coat the chicken with the egg by massaging the bag.
4. Working with one piece of chicken at a time, dredge each piece in the flour mixture, then set on a plate. Let the chicken rest for 3 to 5 minutes; reserve the flour mixture.

5. Check the temperature of the oil in your skillet with an instant-read thermometer. Once it reaches 325°F to 350°F, dredge the chicken again in the flour mixture. (Note: The first dredging of the chicken creates the first layer of batter, while the second dredge adds the crunch factor.)

6. Gently set half the chicken pieces in the hot oil and fry for 2 minutes. Turn each piece with a long-handled strainer or spider and fry for another 5 to 7 minutes, until golden brown and crispy.

7. Transfer the chicken to a plate lined with paper towels. Check the temperature of the chicken. If the chicken is under 165°F, return it to the skillet and continue to cook, flipping the chicken often to ensure even cooking. Move the cooked batch to a sheet pan and place in the warm oven. Continue until all the chicken is fried. Remove the chicken from the oven to briefly toast the benne seeds and biscuits. Increase the oven temperature to 350°F.

The Build

1. Place the benne seeds on a sheet pan and toast in the oven for 10 minutes.

2. Halve the biscuits and place on a parchment paper–lined sheet pan. Toast in the oven for 5 minutes.

3. Place the fried chicken breasts in a large bowl and gently coat with the gochujang honey sauce until well coated.

4. Place the bottom half of a biscuit on a plate and add a piece of fried chicken. Sprinkle with toasted benne seeds, then top with the biscuit lid. Plate the remaining servings.

Kung Pao

The first time I ate kung pao was at a simple Chinese takeout restaurant in Euclid, Ohio. I loved the spice and the combination of citrus and nuts. Kung pao is from the Sichuan region of China, known for its spicy cuisine featuring Sichuan peppercorns and hot chiles. It is one of the top-selling dishes in Chinese restaurants in the United States. Working as a garde-manger under a Malaysian chef named Roy Khoo at the Ritz-Carlton, Amelia Island, I gained a new understanding of Asian cuisine. In creating this dish, I thought about Americans' love of chicken and biscuits and of kung pao, and imagined that anyone would enjoy a marriage of these two delicious dishes.

SERVES 6

INGREDIENTS

FOR THE BRINE
6 (5-ounce) boneless, skinless chicken thighs
1 cup water
1 cup buttermilk
¼ cup apple cider vinegar
3 tablespoons low-sodium soy sauce
¼ cup ground ginger
1 tablespoon kosher salt

FOR THE KUNG PAO SAUCE
½ cup honey
¼ cup low-sodium soy sauce
¼ cup dark soy sauce
1 navel orange, peeled and quartered
2 tablespoons Chinese black vinegar
1 tablespoon sesame oil
1 teaspoon Sichuan peppercorns
1 teaspoon crushed red pepper
½ teaspoon xanthan gum

FOR THE SLAW
½ cup mayonnaise
2 tablespoons granulated sugar
3 tablespoons chopped pickled ginger
1 tablespoon rice vinegar
Kosher salt
8 ounces napa cabbage, shaved (2 cups)
¼ cup shaved purple cabbage
¼ medium red onion, thinly sliced (¼ cup)
¼ cup shredded carrot
¼ bunch cilantro, leaves only (¼ cup)

FOR THE BISCUITS
4 cups self-rising flour, plus more for dusting
1 cup buttermilk
1 cup chopped roasted unsalted peanuts
½ cup granulated sugar
4 tablespoons (½ stick) salted butter, melted
¼ cup smooth peanut butter
2 large eggs
2 tablespoons sesame oil
1 tablespoon apple cider vinegar
1 tablespoon ground ginger
1 tablespoon kosher salt
1 teaspoon xanthan gum

FOR THE DREDGE AND FRY
8 cups canola or corn oil
1 cup self-rising flour
½ cup cornstarch
½ cup rice flour
¼ cup ground ginger
2 large eggs

FOR THE BUILD
¼ cup crushed roasted unsalted peanuts
1 bunch cilantro, leaves only (1 cup)

Brine the Chicken

1. Place the chicken thighs into a 1-gallon resealable plastic bag.
2. In a medium bowl, whisk the water, buttermilk, apple cider vinegar, soy sauce, ground ginger, and salt.
3. Pour the brine into the bag with the chicken thighs and toss with your hands to thoroughly coat the chicken.
4. Seal the bag and place in the refrigerator. Brine for a minimum of 15 minutes and up to 24 hours.

Make the Kung Pao Sauce

1. In a medium saucepan, combine the honey, low-sodium soy sauce, dark soy sauce, navel orange, Chinese black vinegar, sesame oil, Sichuan peppercorns, crushed red pepper, and xanthan gum. Cover and cook over medium-low heat, stirring occasionally, for 20 minutes.
2. Once the orange pieces are soft, puree the sauce with a handheld stick blender until smooth. Strain through a fine-mesh strainer into an airtight container. Reserve. (This sauce can be made ahead. Stored in the refrigerator, it will keep for up to 3 months.)

Make the Slaw

1. In a large bowl, whisk the mayonnaise, sugar, chopped pickled ginger, vinegar, and salt to taste.
2. Add the shaved cabbages, red onion, carrot, and cilantro leaves. Toss together gently until coated. Refrigerate until ready to serve.

Make the Biscuits

1. In a large bowl, mix the flour, buttermilk, peanuts, sugar, butter, peanut butter, eggs, sesame oil, apple cider vinegar, ground ginger, salt, and xanthan gum by hand, just until the dough starts to come together. Alternatively, you can mix the ingredients in the bowl of a stand mixer with the dough hook. Mix on low speed for 2 minutes, just until the dough starts to come together.
2. Line a sheet pan with parchment paper. Using an ice cream scoop, portion out 6 large biscuits. Lightly dust each biscuit with flour and lightly press them down with a spatula or small bowl to a ½-inch thickness.
3. Transfer the sheet pan to the refrigerator and chill the biscuits for at least 15 minutes, or until firm to the touch. Preheat the oven to 375°F.
4. Bake for 15 minutes on the middle rack of the oven. Rotate the sheet pan and bake for another 8 minutes, until the biscuit tops are golden brown. Remove and allow to cool to room temperature. Reduce the oven temperature to 170°F.

Make the Dredge and Fry the Chicken

1. Heat a 14- or 16-inch cast-iron skillet or frying pan on medium-low. Put the oil in the skillet and heat for 20 minutes.
2. Mix the self-rising flour, cornstarch, rice flour, and ground ginger in a large bowl.

3. Remove the bag of brined chicken from the fridge. Whisk the eggs in a small bowl. Add the eggs to the bag, seal, and thoroughly coat the chicken with the egg by massaging the bag.

4. Working with one piece of chicken at a time, dredge each piece in the flour mixture, then set on a plate. Let the chicken rest for 3 to 5 minutes; reserve the flour mixture.

5. Check the temperature of the oil in the skillet with an instant-read thermometer. Once it reaches 325° to 350°F, dredge the chicken again in the flour mixture. (Note: The first dredging of the chicken creates the first layer of batter on the chicken, while the second dredge adds the crunch factor.)

6. Gently set half the chicken pieces in the hot oil and fry for 2 minutes. Turn each piece with a long-handled strainer or spider and fry for another 5 to 7 minutes, until golden brown and crispy.

7. Transfer the chicken to a plate lined with paper towels. Check the temperature of the chicken. If the chicken is under 165°F, return it to the skillet and continue to cook, flipping the chicken often to ensure even cooking. Move the cooked batch to a sheet pan and place in the warm oven. Continue until all the chicken is fried. Remove the chicken from the oven to briefly toast the biscuits. Increase the oven temperature to 400°F.

The Build

1. Halve the biscuits and place on a parchment paper–lined sheet pan. Toast in the oven for 5 minutes.

2. Place the fried chicken in a large bowl and toss with the kung pao sauce until well coated.

3. Place the bottom half of a biscuit on a plate and top with a piece of fried chicken. Add a small scoop of slaw on top of the chicken breast and sprinkle with some crushed roasted peanuts and cilantro leaves. Top with the biscuit lid. Plate the remaining servings and serve the remaining slaw on the side.

Chicken Parmesan

Every global cuisine has its comfort foods that do more than just fill our bellies—they warm our hearts by providing a universal sense of home. Chicken Parmesan is a classic American comfort food created by Italian immigrants—and biscuits are my comfort food. This recipe is a marriage between the two. Southern families pass their biscuit recipes down from generation to generation, and I imagine that Italian American families may do the same with their chicken Parmesan. The drop biscuits featured here incorporate traditional Italian flavors, and would make a wonderful side to any Italian meal.

INGREDIENTS

SERVES 6

FOR THE MARINARA SAUCE
Make 6 cups
½ cup extra-virgin olive oil
2 small Spanish onions, finely diced (1 cup)
6 cloves garlic, peeled
Pinch of crushed red pepper
2 cups canned diced tomatoes (about two-thirds
    of a 28-ounce can)
1 bunch basil, leaves only (1 cup)
½ medium red bell pepper, seeded and diced
    (½ cup)
Juice of 1 lemon
1 teaspoon kosher salt

FOR THE BISCUITS
4 cups self-rising flour, plus more for dusting
1 cup buttermilk
1 bunch basil, chopped (1 cup)
3½ ounces Asiago cheese, grated (1 cup)
½ cup granulated sugar
4 tablespoons (½ stick) salted butter, melted
¼ cup vegetable shortening
2 large eggs
¼ cup granulated garlic
3 tablespoons extra-virgin olive oil
1 tablespoon apple cider vinegar
1 tablespoon crushed red pepper
1 tablespoon kosher salt
1 teaspoon xanthan gum

FOR THE BREADED CHICKEN
6 (5-ounce) boneless, skinless chicken breasts
½ cup extra-virgin olive oil
1 tablespoon granulated garlic
1 teaspoon kosher salt
1 cup buttermilk
6 large eggs
3 cups self-rising flour
3 cups Italian-style breadcrumbs

FOR THE FRY
8 cups canola or corn oil

FOR THE BUILD
12 slices fresh mozzarella cheese
12 fresh basil leaves
¼ cup grated Parmesan cheese

DIRECTIONS

Make the Marinara Sauce

1. Warm a medium saucepan over medium heat and add the olive oil, onions, garlic, and crushed red pepper and cook for 10 minutes, stirring occasionally.
2. Add the remaining ingredients and bring to a simmer. Cook for an additional 10 minutes.
3. Puree the mixture with a handheld stick blender until smooth. Rewarm when ready to serve. (Store leftovers in an airtight containter in the refrigerator for up to 1 week or freeze for up to 30 days. Use with pasta or as a dipping sauce for crusty bread or grilled veggies.)

Make the Biscuits

1. In a large bowl, mix the flour, buttermilk, basil, Asiago cheese, sugar, melted butter, shortening, eggs, granulated garlic, olive oil, apple cider vinegar, crushed red pepper, salt, and xanthan gum by hand, just until the dough starts to come together. Alternatively, you can mix the ingredients in the bowl of a stand mixer with the dough hook. Mix on low speed for 2 minutes. Scrape the bowl and mix for another minute, just until the dough starts to come together.
2. Line a sheet pan with parchment paper. Using an ice cream scoop, portion out 6 large biscuits. Lightly dust each biscuit with flour and lightly press them down with a spatula or small bowl to a ½-inch thickness.
3. Transfer the sheet pan to the refrigerator and chill the biscuits for at least 15 minutes, or until firm to the touch. Preheat the oven to 375°F.
4. Bake for 15 minutes on the middle rack of the oven. Rotate the sheet pan and bake for another 8 minutes, until the biscuit tops are golden brown. Remove and allow to cool to room temperature. Reduce the oven temperature to 170°F.

Make the Breaded Chicken

1. Cover the surface of a large cutting board with plastic wrap and place the chicken breasts on top. Lay another piece of plastic wrap flat over the chicken, sandwiching the breasts between the two pieces. Using a mallet, pound the chicken breasts until they are about ¼ inch thick.
2. Whisk the olive oil, garlic, and salt in a large bowl. Add the chicken breasts and toss until coated.
3. Whisk the buttermilk and eggs in a medium bowl. Put the flour and breadcrumbs into separate medium bowls.
4. Line a sheet pan with parchment paper. Line up the bowls on your counter in the following sequence: flour, egg-buttermilk mixture, breadcrumbs.
5. Working with one piece of chicken at a time, dip the chicken in the flour, then the egg-buttermilk mixture, then the breadcrumbs. Coat the chicken on all surfaces. Place on the parchment paper–lined sheet pan and coat the remaining pieces.

Fry the Chicken

1. Heat a 14- or 16-inch cast-iron skillet or frying pan on medium-low. Place the oil in the skillet and heat for 20 minutes.

2. Check the temperature of the oil in your skillet with an instant-read thermometer. Once it reaches 325° to 350°F, gently set half the chicken pieces in the hot oil and fry for 2 minutes. Turn each piece with a long-handled strainer or spider and fry for another 5 to 7 minutes, until golden brown and crispy.

3. Transfer the chicken to a plate lined with paper towels. Check the temperature of the chicken. If the chicken is under 165°F, return it to the skillet and continue to cook, flipping the chicken often to ensure even cooking.

4. Move the cooked batch to a sheet pan and place in the warm oven. Continue until all the chicken is fried. Remove the chicken from the oven to briefly toast the biscuits. Increase the oven temperature to 400°F.

The Build

1. Halve the biscuits and place on a parchment paper–lined sheet pan. Toast in the oven for 5 minutes. Keep the oven on.

2. Place the fried chicken on a second sheet pan lined with parchment paper.

3. Top each piece of chicken with 2 to 4 tablespoons of marinara sauce, 2 slices of mozzarella, and 2 basil leaves.

4. Bake for 5 minutes, or until the cheese is melted and bubbling.

5. Place the bottom half of a biscuit on a plate and top with 1 tablespoon of marinara, then add a piece of chicken. Sprinkle the chicken with parmesan cheese and top with the biscuit lid. Plate the remaining servings.

MEATLOAF

+ MASHED POTATOES

BACON-WRAPPED MEATLOAF WITH
SOUR CREAM MASHED POTATOES

Beef meatloaf wrapped in smoky bacon and glazed with chipotle ketchup,
served on sour cream–enriched mashed potatoes and topped
with tasso ham gravy and roasted broccoli

56

SHAWARMA-SPICED LAMB MEATLOAF WITH
FETA AND KALAMATA MASHED POTATOES

Minced lamb meatloaf with Middle Eastern spices served on
feta cheese and kalamata olive mashed potatoes with a tomato-cucumber
salad and lemon-garlic sauce

62

TURKEY MEATLOAF WITH MOROCCAN SPICES AND
CASHEW-CAULIFLOWER MASH

Ground dark- and white-meat turkey seasoned with Moroccan spices,
served with a cashew and cauliflower mash and roasted cauliflower
wedges, drizzled with preserved Moroccan lemon butter, and finished
with a scattering of pickled golden raisins and fresh dill

66

ITALIAN MEATLOAF WITH WHITE TRUFFLE AND
MASCARPONE MASHED POTATOES

Garlicky rosemary-infused beef, veal, and pork meatloaf with
ricotta cheese and Italian breadcrumbs served with
truffle-mascarpone mashed potatoes and sage-mushroom gravy
with roasted baby carrots and Tuscan kale

70

When I was young, it was rare for my family to sit in front of the TV and eat a meal. My mom limited the TV time of my younger brother and I—our days were all about playing outside with friends, building forts, doing sports, hiking, and swimming at the local pool. And dinner was always enjoyed at the table.

As we got older, our schedules became busier and dinner became more flexible. On the evenings when my dad was at work, my mom would have dinner warming on the stove for us to eat when we got home. We would make our own plates, sit on the sofa, and watch TV. We watched *All in the Family*, *The Jeffersons*, *M*A*S*H*, *Mork & Mindy*, and sometimes we would eat in our bedrooms if we had homework to do.

Meatloaf and mashed potatoes take me back to those chill nights at home. Mom would serve the dish with a basic vegetable prepared with salt, pepper, and a little bit of butter. Sometimes she would cheat and use a can of mixed vegetables, but the mashed potatoes were always fresh. She only used russet potatoes, which she would peel with a paring knife. Her meatloaf was simple: ground beef, peppers, onions, garlic, salt, eggs, and breadcrumbs. She would glaze the meatloaf with ketchup, which would caramelize in the oven as it baked.

Most classic meatloaf is like my mom's recipe, where the onions and peppers are chopped and folded into the meat. Each bite contains a little piece of diced vegetable. I do meatloaf a little differently. I puree the vegetables and eggs together and then knead them into the meat with breadcrumbs. This method allows for every bite to be flavored with all the vegetables, versus a bite with a little onion and another with a bit of diced pepper.

Great flavor and moisture are what make a meatloaf outstanding. You can use many different types of meat, but the protein-to-fat ratio is important to keep it tender and delicious. I like an 80 percent protein to 20 percent fat ratio, and ground chuck is my preferred meat. It comes from the shoulder of the cow, so it contains more fat.

Meatloaf and mashed potatoes is as American a dish as can be, and it is easy to experiment with this classic. The components in any meatloaf are usually the same: protein in the form of ground pork, beef, turkey, lamb, veal, chicken, or a combination, plus vegetables, eggs, and breadcrumbs. Different families in America use different spices, breads, and ground meats at home. If the essential elements are there, meatloaf can be adapted to fit any family's dinner table . . . or sofa. It is a dish that makes for delicious leftovers. Cook it on a Sunday, and you have Monday night's dinner covered too.

Bacon-Wrapped Meatloaf with Sour Cream Mashed Potatoes

This meatloaf features a cravable flavor combinations: The smoky bacon adds flavor and richness due to its fat, the chipotle ketchup builds on that smokiness, and the Boursin cheese melts into the meat, leaving garlic and herb notes. The gravy, made from Cajun-spiced tasso ham, ties it all together.

SERVES 6

FOR THE MEATLOAF

2 pounds sliced smoked bacon

6 large eggs

½ medium red bell pepper, seeded and cut into large dice (½ cup)

½ medium yellow or white onion, cut into large dice (½ cup)

2 medium ribs celery, cut into large dice (½ cup)

5 cloves garlic, peeled

2 tablespoons Chef Kenny's Raging Cajun Spice, or other Cajun seasoning

1 tablespoon kosher salt

¼ bunch flat-leaf parsley, leaves chopped (¼ cup)

2 pounds (80/20) ground beef

8 ounces garlic-and-herb Boursin cheese

3 cups panko breadcrumbs

FOR THE CHIPOTLE KETCHUP
Makes 6 cups

1 (28-ounce can) crushed tomatoes, preferably San Marzano (3 cups)

1 cup apple cider vinegar

1 cup packed light brown sugar

¼ cup canned chipotle in adobo sauce (3 chipotles plus sauce)

1 tablespoon ground cumin

1 tablespoon kosher salt

1 teaspoon xanthan gum

FOR THE MASHED POTATOES

12 to 14 medium Red Bliss or other medium red potatoes, coarsely diced (6 cups)

4 tablespoons (½ stick) salted butter

1 tablespoon kosher salt

1 cup sour cream

FOR THE TASSO HAM GRAVY

¼ cup corn oil

¼ cup all-purpose flour

8 ounces ground tasso ham, ground chorizo, or ground bacon

¼ red bell pepper, seeded and cut into large dice (¼ cup)

1 medium rib celery, cut into large dice (¼ cup)

½ small Spanish onion, cut into large dice (¼ cup)

5 cloves garlic

2 cups water

1 tablespoon Chef Kenny's Raging Cajun Spice, or other Cajun seasoning

1 tablespoon chicken bouillon powder, preferably Knorr

1 teaspoon kosher salt

1 cup heavy cream

4 bay leaves

FOR THE ROASTED BROCCOLI

1 small to medium head broccoli, florets only (2 cups)

¼ cup extra-virgin olive oil

1 tablespoon Chef Kenny's Fried Chicken Seasoning, or other poultry seasoning

Pinch of kosher salt

Make the Meatloaf

1. Preheat the oven to 375°F and line a large (8½ x 4½-inch) loaf pan with the bacon. Place the loaf pan on a sheet pan.
2. Put the eggs, bell pepper, onion, celery, garlic, Cajun seasoning, salt, and parsley in a blender and puree until smooth. Transfer this egg-vegetable puree to a large bowl.
3. Add the ground beef, Boursin cheese, and breadcrumbs to the bowl. Mix thoroughly with your hands.
4. Fill the prepared loaf pan with the meatloaf mixture and fold the overhanging bacon over the meatloaf. Bake for 45 minutes, then rotate the pan and bake for another 25 minutes, until the meatloaf reaches an internal temperature of 155°F.
5. Allow the meatloaf to rest for 20 minutes. Unmold by gently turning over the loaf pan and easing it out onto the sheet pan.
6. Preheat the broiler. Broil the meatloaf on the bottom rack until the bacon crisps, about 5 minutes. Set aside.

Make the Chipotle Ketchup

1. In a medium saucepan on medium heat, simmer the tomatoes, apple cider vinegar, brown sugar, chipotles in adobo, cumin, salt, and xanthan gum. Stir occasionally to ensure that the sugars do not caramelize on the bottom of the pan.
2. Reduce the heat to low and cook for 20 minutes, or until the ketchup has reduced by half and thickened.
3. Remove from the heat and puree the mixture with a handheld stick blender until smooth.
4. Let cool, then transfer to an airtight container and refrigerate until ready to use. (This ketchup can be made ahead and stored in the refrigerator for up to 12 months. It is delicious with french fries, and also as an alternative any other time you use ketchup.)

Make the Mashed Potatoes

1. Put the potatoes into a medium saucepan and cover with cold water. Bring to a boil over high heat.
2. Reduce the heat to medium and simmer the potatoes for 20 minutes, until fork-tender.
3. Drain the potatoes, return them to the saucepan, and add the butter and salt.
4. Use a potato masher to evenly crush the potatoes. Add the sour cream and mash until well blended, creamy, and fluffy. Cover and keep warm until ready to serve.

Make the Tasso Ham Gravy

1. Cook the corn oil and flour in a small saucepan over medium heat, stirring regularly with a wooden spoon or whisk for 8 to 10 minutes, until a pecan-colored roux develops.
2. Add the ground tasso ham and cook, stirring occasionally, until the fat renders and the meat resembles crispy brown bacon bits.
3. Put the bell pepper, celery, onion, garlic, water, Cajun seasoning, bouillon, and salt into a blender and puree until smooth.
4. Pour the vegetable mixture into the pot with the tasso ham and add the cream and bay leaves.

5. Bring the mixture to a boil, then reduce the heat to maintain a simmer. Cook for 20 minutes, stirring regularly, until the consistency of buttermilk. Off the heat, remove and discard the bay leaves and skim the starches that have risen to the top. Set aside the gravy.

Make the Broccoli

1. Preheat the broiler and line a sheet pan with foil.
2. Gently toss the broccoli with the olive oil and chicken seasoning in a medium bowl, then transfer the broccoli to the prepared sheet pan. Set on the middle rack of the oven.
3. Broil for 5 minutes, until charred. Remove from the oven, but keep the broiler on. Sprinkle the charred broccoli with the salt.

The Build

1. Line a sheet pan with foil and spray with Pam or olive oil pan spray.
2. Cut 6 slices of meatloaf. Set the slices on the prepared sheet pan and top each slice with 1 or 2 tablespoons of the chipotle ketchup.
3. Broil the meatloaf slices on the middle rack for 1 to 2 minutes, or until the ketchup caramelizes.
4. Place a large scoop of mashed potatoes on a plate. Top the potatoes with a slice of meatloaf. Spoon tasso ham gravy over the meatloaf and potatoes and add a few broccoli florets. Plate the remaining servings. Serve any remaining mashed potatoes and broccoli on the side.

Shawarma-Spiced Lamb Meatloaf with Feta and Kalamata Mashed Potatoes

Not all families in America enjoy beef. We are a nation of many people and cultures, and for some, beef is just not on the table. This meatloaf recipe calls for lamb and is designed to allow families who don't eat beef to still be able to dig into this iconic American dish. Not all families have a loaf of wheat or Wonder bread on the shelf at home either. Here we use pita for the breadcrumb component, because why not?

INGREDIENTS

SERVES 6

FOR THE LEMON-GARLIC SAUCE
Makes 3 cups

1 cup sour cream
1 cup whole-milk plain Greek yogurt
1 bunch cilantro, chopped (1 cup)
Juice of 3 or 4 lemons (½ cup)
10 cloves garlic, peeled
1 tablespoon ground cumin
1 tablespoon ground coriander
1 tablespoon kosher salt

FOR THE TOMATO-CUCUMBER SALAD

½ cup extra-virgin olive oil
Juice of 1 lime
Juice of 1 lemon
1 tablespoon ground sumac
1 teaspoon ground cumin
Pinch of kosher salt, or to taste
Pinch of freshly ground black pepper
4 ounces baby kale leaves (2 loosely packed cups), preferably Tuscan
5 ounces cherry tomatoes, halved (1 cup)
½ medium seedless English cucumber, unpeeled and diced (1 cup)
6 to 8 radishes, quartered (1 cup)
½ medium red onion, sliced (½ cup)
¼ bunch mint, chopped (¼ cup)
¼ bunch cilantro, chopped (¼ cup)
¼ cup chopped pitted Kalamata olives

FOR THE MEATLOAF

6 large eggs
½ red bell pepper, seeded and cut into large dice (½ cup)
1 small Spanish onion, cut into large dice (½ cup)
2 ribs celery, cut into large dice (½ cup)
¼ bunch cilantro, chopped (¼ cup)
¼ bunch mint, leaves only (¼ cup)
5 cloves garlic, peeled
2 tablespoons Chef Kenny's Cinnamon Coffee Rub (to make your own, see page 16)
1 tablespoon Chef Kenny's Fried Chicken Seasoning, or other poultry seasoning
1 tablespoon kosher salt
2 teaspoons ground cardamom
1 teaspoon ground sumac
2 pounds ground lamb
8 ounces goat cheese
3 pitas, finely chopped into crumbs (3 cups)

FOR THE MASHED POTATOES

1½ pounds medium red potatoes or coarsely diced peeled Yukon Gold or russet potatoes (6 cups)
4 tablespoons (½ stick) salted butter
1 tablespoon kosher salt
1 cup sour cream
5¼ ounces feta cheese, crumbled (1 cup)
¼ cup chopped pitted Kalamata olives
¼ bunch flat-leaf parsley, leaves chopped (¼ cup)
Extra-virgin olive oil, for drizzling

Make the Lemon-Garlic Sauce

1. Puree the sour cream, Greek yogurt, cilantro, lemon juice, garlic, cumin, coriander, and salt in a food processor or blender until smooth.
2. Transfer to an airtight container and refrigerate until ready to use. When ready to serve, transfer to a dish. (This sauce can be made up to 1 week ahead. Leftover sauce can be used as a dip for crudités or to dress a salad, or added to tuna fish to make tuna salad.)

Make the Tomato-Cucumber Salad

1. In a large bowl, whisk the olive oil, lime and lemon juices, sumac, cumin, salt, and black pepper.
2. Add the kale, tomatoes, cucumber, radishes, onion, mint, cilantro, and olives and gently toss together. Set aside until ready to serve.

Make the Meatloaf

1. Preheat the oven to 375°F and put a large (8½ x 4½-inch) loaf pan on a sheet pan.
2. Put the eggs, bell pepper, onion, celery, cilantro, mint, garlic, coffee rub, chicken seasoning, salt, cardamom, and sumac in a blender and puree until smooth. Transfer this egg-vegetable puree to a large bowl.
3. Add the ground lamb, goat cheese, and pita breadcrumbs. Mix thoroughly with your hands.
4. Fill the loaf pan with the meatloaf mixture. Bake for 45 minutes, then rotate the pan and bake for another 25 minutes, or until the meatloaf reaches an internal temperature of 155°F.
5. Allow the meatloaf to rest for 20 minutes. Unmold the meatloaf by gently turning over the loaf pan and easing it out onto a cutting board. Cut into 6 slices.

Make the Mashed Potatoes

1. Put the potatoes in a medium saucepan and cover with cold water. Bring to a boil over high heat.
2. Reduce the heat to medium and simmer the potatoes for 20 minutes, or until fork-tender.
3. Drain the potatoes, return them to the saucepan, and add the butter and salt.
4. Use a potato masher to evenly crush the potatoes. Add the sour cream, feta cheese, olives, and parsley to the potatoes and mash them until well blended and the potatoes are creamy and fluffy. Cover and keep warm until ready to serve. When ready to serve, drizzle with some olive oil.

The Build

Place a large scoop of mashed potatoes on a dinner plate and top with a slice of meatloaf. Spoon the sauce over the meatloaf and add a generous helping of salad. Plate the remaining servings. Serve any remaining mashed potatoes, sauce, and salad on the side.

Turkey Meatloaf with Moroccan Spices and Cashew-Cauliflower Mash

Turkey is a great beef substitute if you are looking to add a leaner meatloaf to the rotation. Because turkey has less fat, it has a milder flavor. When cooking with ground turkey, it is a good idea to bump up the flavor with bold spices. The Moroccan spices in this dish—turmeric, ginger, paprika, cumin, and coriander, to name a few from a spice blend—are so flavorful. This meatloaf is terrific—a healthier alternative and packed with flavor. Preserved lemons are a staple of Morrocan cuisine; note that the lemons in this dish need to be made at least 12 hours in advance.

INGREDIENTS

SERVES 6

FOR THE PICKLED RAISINS
½ cup apple cider vinegar
1 teaspoon crushed red pepper
½ cup golden raisins
½ cup black raisins

FOR THE PICKLED LEMONS
1 cup granulated sugar
1 cup apple cider vinegar
2 tablespoons kosher salt
4 lemons, quartered

FOR THE PICKLED LEMON-BUTTER SAUCE
1 cup (2 sticks) salted butter
½ cup seeded and finely chopped Pickled Lemons (see above)
4 cloves garlic, minced
1 tablespoon Chef Kenny's Moroccan Spice, or other Moroccan spice blend

FOR THE MEATLOAF
6 large eggs
½ medium red bell pepper, seeded and cut into large dice (½ cup)
1 small Spanish onion, cut into large dice (½ cup)
2 medium ribs celery, cut into large dice (½ cup)
¼ bunch dill, chopped (¼ cup)
¼ bunch flat-leaf parsley, leaves chopped (¼ cup)
5 cloves garlic, peeled

3 tablespoons Chef Kenny's Moroccan Spice, or other Moroccan spice blend
1 tablespoon kosher salt
2 pounds ground turkey (preferably a mix of dark and white meat)
3 cups panko breadcrumbs
1 cup heavy cream
2 ounces soft goat cheese (½ cup)

FOR THE MASHED POTATOES
½ cup raw cashews
3 peeled russet potatoes, coarsely diced (3 cups)
1 small head cauliflower, florets only (3 cups)
1 cup cashew or almond milk
4 tablespoons (½ stick) salted butter
1 tablespoon kosher salt

FOR THE ROASTED CAULIFLOWER
1 medium head cauliflower, cut into wedges
¼ cup extra-virgin olive oil
2 tablespoons Chef Kenny's Moroccan Spice, or other Moroccan spice blend
Pinch of kosher salt

FOR THE BUILD
Fresh dill, for garnish

**Make the
Pickled Raisins**

1. Boil the vinegar and crushed red pepper in a small saucepan on high heat.
2. Put the raisins in a small bowl and pour the hot vinegar over them. Soak for at least 1 hour or up to 24 hours.

**Make the
Pickled Lemons**

1. Cook the sugar, vinegar, and salt in a medium saucepan over low heat, just until the sugar and salt dissolve.
2. Put the lemon quarters in a heat-safe airtight container and pour the hot sugar-vinegar mixture over them. Cover and store overnight in the refrigerator. (The pickled lemons can be made well in advance, and they will keep in the refrigerator for up to 12 months. You can use pickled lemons in dressings, salads, and marinades.)

**Make the Pickled
Lemon–Butter Sauce**

1. Melt the butter in a small saucepan on medium heat. Add the pickled lemons, garlic, and Moroccan spice blend.
2. Reduce the heat to low and cook for 5 minutes, stirring occasionally. Remove from the heat and cover to keep warm until ready to serve.

Make the Meatloaf

1. Preheat the oven to 375°F and put a large (8½ x 4½-inch) loaf pan on a sheet pan.
2. Place the eggs, bell pepper, onion, celery, dill, parsley, garlic, Moroccan spice blend, and salt in a blender and puree until smooth. Transfer this egg-vegetable puree to the bowl of a stand mixer with dough hook.
3. Add the ground turkey, breadcrumbs, heavy cream, and goat cheese to the mixer bowl. Mix on low speed until well combined, about 1 minute.
4. Fill the loaf pan with the meatloaf mixture. Bake for 45 minutes, then rotate the pan and bake for another 25 minutes, or until the meatloaf reaches an internal temperature of 155°F. Remove from the oven and reduce the oven temperature to 350°F.
5. Allow the meatloaf to rest for 20 minutes. Unmold by gently turning over the loaf pan and easing it out onto a cutting board. Cut into 6 slices.

**Make the
Mashed Potatoes**

1. Place the cashews on a small sheet pan and toast in the oven for 10 minutes, or until fragrant. Allow to cool, then grind in a food processor. Set aside.
2. Put the potatoes and cauliflower in a large saucepan and cover with cold water. Bring to a boil over high heat, then reduce the heat to medium. Simmer for 20 minutes, or until the potatoes and cauliflower are fork-tender.
3. Warm the nut milk and ground cashews in a small saucepan over low heat.
4. Drain the potatoes and cauliflower, return them to the saucepan, and add the butter and salt. Use a potato masher to evenly crush the potatoes and cauliflower, then whisk until smooth. Add the warm nut milk mixture and whisk until incorporated. Cover to keep warm until ready to serve.

Make the Roasted Cauliflower

1. Preheat the broiler and line a sheet pan with foil.
2. In a large bowl, gently toss the cauliflower with the olive oil and Moroccan seasoning. Arrange the cauliflower on the prepared sheet pan.
3. Broil on the middle rack for 5 minutes, or until the wedges are caramelized. Season the cauliflower with the salt.

The Build

1. Place a large scoop of mashed potatoes on a dinner plate and lay a slice of meatloaf on top. Add wedges of roasted cauliflower.
2. Top the meatloaf and cauliflower with a large spoonful of pickled lemon–butter sauce.
3. Garnish with pickled raisins and lots of fresh dill. Plate the remaining servings and serve the remaining mashed potatoes, sauce, and cauliflower on the side.

Italian Meatloaf with White Truffle and Mascarpone Mashed Potatoes

Here is a secret tip: You can make meatballs from any meatloaf recipe. Meatballs and meatloaf are essentially the same, except for their shape and that meatloaf usually has a glaze. This recipe makes an Italian-style meatloaf from a combination of beef, veal, pork, and ricotta cheese, and it is delicious. You can also use it if you are looking for a great meatball to go with your spaghetti. If you don't have the time to bake a loaf, roll the meat into golf ball–sized balls and bake them off for 20 minutes at 375°F. Meatballs are a great quick protein to cook up on a busy weeknight.

SERVES 6

INGREDIENTS

FOR THE SAGE-MUSHROOM GRAVY
¼ cup extra-virgin olive oil
¼ cup all-purpose flour
8 ounces portobello mushrooms, chopped (2⅔ cups)
½ cup Marsala wine
2 cups water or vegetable broth
¼ cup fennel, coarsely chopped
¼ medium yellow or white onion, coarsely chopped (¼ cup)
12 fresh sage leaves
5 cloves garlic, peeled
1 tablespoon granulated vegetable bouillon
1 cup heavy cream
1 teaspoon kosher salt

FOR THE MEATLOAF
6 large eggs
½ red bell pepper, seeded and cut into large dice (½ cup)
1 small Spanish onion, cut into large dice (½ cup)
2 ribs celery, cut into large dice (½ cup)
½ cup peeled garlic cloves (10 to 12 cloves)
2 to 3 sprigs rosemary, leaves only, chopped (¼ cup)
1 tablespoon kosher salt
1 pound (80/20) ground beef

8 ounces ground veal
8 ounces ground pork
1 cup ricotta cheese
3 cups Italian-style breadcrumbs

FOR THE MASHED POTATOES
6 peeled medium russet potatoes, coarsely diced (6 cups)
4 tablespoons (½ stick) salted butter
1 tablespoon kosher salt
1 cup mascarpone cheese
1 tablespoon white truffle oil
1 tablespoon kosher salt

FOR THE KALE AND YOUNG CARROTS
1 pound peeled young carrots
¼ cup extra-virgin olive oil
8 ounces Tuscan kale or baby kale
Pinch of kosher salt
Zest of 1 lemon
1 teaspoon crushed red pepper

**Make the
Sage-Mushroom Gravy**

1. Mix the olive oil and flour in a small saucepan. Cook on medium heat, stirring regularly, for 10 to 15 minutes, until a pecan-colored roux develops.
2. Add the mushrooms and cook, stirring occasionally, until tender, about 3 minutes.
3. Pour in the Marsala and scrape the brown bits on the bottom of the pan. Cook for about 30 seconds. Turn off the heat.
4. Put the water, fennel, onion, sage, garlic, and bouillon in a blender and puree until smooth.
5. Pour the puree into the pot with the mushrooms and add the cream. Stir, then turn the heat to high and bring the mixture to a boil. Reduce the heat to maintain a simmer, and simmer for 25 minutes, skimming off the starches as they rise to the top of the pot. Add the salt, stir, and remove from heat. Cover to keep warm.

Make the Meatloaf

1. Preheat the oven to 375°F and put a large (8½ x 4½-inch) loaf pan on a sheet pan.
2. Put the eggs, bell pepper, onion, celery, garlic, rosemary, and salt in a blender and puree until smooth. Transfer to a large bowl.
3. Add the ground beef, veal, and pork, the ricotta, and breadcrumbs to the bowl with the egg-vegetable puree. Mix thoroughly with your hands.
4. Fill the loaf pan with the meatloaf mixture. Bake for 45 minutes, then rotate the pan and bake for another 25 minutes, or until the meatloaf reaches an internal temperature of 155°F.
5. Allow the meatloaf to rest for 20 minutes. Unmold by gently turning over the loaf pan and easing it out onto a cutting board. Cut into 6 slices.

**Make the
Mashed Potatoes**

1. Put the potatoes in a medium saucepan and cover with cold water. Bring to a boil over high heat, then reduce the heat to medium and simmer for 20 minutes, or until fork-tender.
2. Drain the potatoes, return them to the saucepan, and add the butter and salt. Use a potato masher to evenly crush the potatoes. Add the mascarpone and truffle oil to the mashed potatoes. Incorporate until the potatoes are creamy and fluffy. Cover to keep warm until ready to serve.

**Make the Kale
and Young Carrots**

1. Preheat the broiler and line a sheet pan with foil.
2. In a large bowl, toss the carrots with half of the olive oil and arrange on the prepared sheet pan. Broil on the middle rack for 5 minutes, until browned; transfer to a plate or bowl. Repeat with the kale.
3. Once the vegetables are roasted, sprinkle with the salt, lemon zest, and crushed red pepper.

The Build

Assemble family style: Place each component of the meal in its own serving dish and arrange around the table so guests can make their own plates.

RIBS + SLAW

CARLE ANTHONY'S ST. LOUIS RIBS WITH CARLOTTA'S CREAMY SLAW

Spice-rubbed smoked St. Louis ribs glazed with
Sweet Tomato–Molasses BBQ Sauce, served on white bread
with a side of my mother's flavor-packed slaw

80

COFFEE-RUBBED SPARERIBS WITH POBLANO-APPLE SLAW

South-of-the-border smoked pork spareribs lacquered
with Espresso BBQ Sauce, served with flour tortillas and
a gently spiced poblano-apple slaw

84

JERK-SPICED SPARERIBS WITH COCONUT GUAVA SLAW

Smoky and spicy jerk spice–rubbed spareribs glazed with
a spicy-sweet Habanero-Mango BBQ Sauce and
served with a cooling coconut and guava slaw

88

WASABI, HONEY, AND SOY-GLAZED BABY BACK RIBS WITH PINEAPPLE, JICAMA, AND PICKLED GINGER SLAW

Oven-roasted baby back ribs rubbed with a
simple ginger rub, then laced with a wasabi-honey soy sauce
and served with a refreshing slaw featuring pineapple,
jicama, and pickled ginger

92

When I make ribs, I always think of my father. Dad was an insurance salesman, and how he presented himself was important to him. Every weekday he wore a full three-piece suit, dress socks, polished shoes, and a hat. His undershirts and underwear were silk, and his nails were always manicured. He dressed sharp and worked hard. During the week, he killed it in sales, and every weekend, he would barbecue.

He and his good friend Eddie Jones would wake up early and spend the day grilling or smoking meat in our backyard or over at Eddie's house. We had a Weber grill and an oil drum pit smoker. Dad would wear his white undershirt, shorts, sandals or house shoes with dress socks pulled up to his calves, and a fedora-style hat. He tended the grill and smoker out on the back patio throughout the day, smoking ribs and chicken or grilling hot dogs and burgers.

My dad grew up on the South Side of Chicago, and he liked the flavor of Kansas City barbecue sauce but didn't like it too thick. His ribs were about the cooking process, not the sauce.

Dad would pull the meat out of the cooler hours in advance to bring it up to room temperature. This would allow his seasoning rub to penetrate the meat better. The last hour of cooking, he would take his sauce and mop the ribs with it. It would cook into the meat, but not create a sticky and tacky coat. It would form a light glaze and keep the meat moist. He usually cooked a St. Louis–style rib—trimmed full slabs that have the tips and brisket removed—or he would buy big spareribs, cut the tips off, and cook the tips up with his homemade sauce. We would eat them as a snack while he was grilling the spareribs. Sometimes, he would cook them Western-style. Western-style ribs are almost like a pork butt. Dad would season them up and fry them almost like he was cooking pork chops. Then he would toss them in his tomato-molasses barbecue sauce. That was my favorite.

Like so many home cooks, my dad's sauce was a mixture of other sauces: Open Pit, ketchup, molasses, mustard, and a few others. When I was eight years old, my dad taught me how to fire up the grill, but it wasn't until my twenties that he shared his barbecue sauce recipe. I was a sous chef at the Ritz-Carlton Grill Room, and my dad came to visit. He had dinner off the menu, but I also made him some lamb ribs as a special dish. After that meal, he wrote down his barbecue sauce recipe on an insurance envelope that I still have to this day. He had passed the torch.

Carle Anthony's St. Louis Ribs with Carlotta's Creamy Slaw

My mom had a rule on weeknights: If we filled our plates with food, we had to eat everything we took. My dad had a rule on weekends: If we took ribs off the grill, we better clean them to the bone. Dad worked the grill and smoker in the backyard, and Mom would make slaw, or macaroni or potato salad as sides. Dad would check in with her for the final say on dinner. She would taste the sauce, the ribs, or the smoked chicken for seasoning. If it was good, she would say, "That's the one right there," but if it wasn't right, she wouldn't say exactly what was needed—she would just hint that it wasn't where it should be. My dad inspired my rib recipe, and my slaw is from my mother. Ribs and slaw take me back to those weekends with my family, slowing down and enjoying life together.

INGREDIENTS

SERVES 6

FOR THE SWEET TOMATO-MOLASSES BBQ SAUCE
Makes 8 cups

4 cups ketchup

2 cups apple cider vinegar

1 cup molasses

1 cup packed light brown sugar

Juice of 2 navel oranges (½ cup)

Juice of 2 lemons (¼ cup)

2 tablespoons Chef Kenny's Raging Cajun Spice, or other Cajun seasoning

2 tablespoons Chef Kenny's Fried Chicken Seasoning, or other poultry seasoning

1 tablespoon whole black peppercorns

1 tablespoon kosher salt

1 teaspoon crushed red pepper

FOR THE RIBS

3 slabs St. Louis–style ribs

½ cup Chef Kenny's Raging Cajun Spice, or other Cajun spice blend

3 cups Sweet Tomato-Molasses BBQ Sauce (see above)

FOR THE SLAW

1 cup mayonnaise

½ cup granulated sugar

¼ cup apple cider vinegar

Kosher salt

1 head white cabbage, grated (6 cups)

¼ cup grated purple cabbage

¼ cup grated carrot

¼ cup dill pickle relish

1 teaspoon Chef Kenny's Raging Cajun Spice, or other Cajun seasoning

FOR THE BUILD

6 slices Wonder or other white bread

Make the Sweet Tomato-Molasses Barbecue Sauce

In a large bowl, combine the ketchup, apple cider vinegar, molasses, brown sugar, orange and lemon juices, Cajun spice blend, chicken seasoning, peppercorns, salt, and crushed red pepper. Whisk to blend, then set aside. (The sauce keeps for up to 12 months, stored in an airtight container in the refrigerator.)

Make the Ribs

1. Preheat a smoker with charcoal and hickory wood to 275° or 300°F, or preheat the oven to 300°F.
2. Season the ribs on both sides with the Cajun seasoning.
3. Place the ribs in the smoker directly on the grate, backbone side down, and cook for 1½ to 2 hours, or until they reach an internal temperature of 165°F. Keep the smoker on. If cooking in the oven, put the ribs on sheet pans lined with foil and cook for 1½ to 2 hours, or until they reach an internal temperature of 165°F. Keep the oven on.
4. Transfer each of the slabs to a large sheet of foil, backbone side down. Pour 1 cup barbecue sauce over each slab, then wrap them in the foil.
5. Return the ribs to the smoker or oven and cook for another 1¼ hours, or until they reach an internal temperature of 195°F.
6. Rest the foil-wrapped cooked ribs in a cooler (without ice) for a minimum of 30 minutes and a maximum of 3 hours before serving.

Make the Slaw

Whisk the mayonnaise, sugar, vinegar, and salt to taste in a large bowl. Add the white cabbage, purple cabbage, carrot, pickle relish, and Cajun seasoning and toss well. Store in the refrigerator until ready to serve.

The Build

1. Using a sharp chef's knife, cut the slabs of ribs into three-rib portions. Be sure to cut close to the bone of the next rib; that way every rib will have meat on the bone.
2. Place a slice of bread on a plate. Top with three ribs. Place barbecue sauce in a small cup on one side of the bread and slaw on the other side. Repeat for the remaining servings.

Coffee-Rubbed Spareribs with Poblano Apple Slaw

I worked with a chef from the Big Island of Hawaii many moons ago. One day on the job, he shared with me a Kona coffee rub that he grew up eating in Hawaii. He used his coffee rub on a rack of lamb, and I remember how beautiful the flavors were. I began to play with it, and instead of using Kona coffee, I tried it with a Colombian and Costa Rican blend. I felt like it really lent itself to Spanish flavors, like poblano peppers, cumin, cinnamon, and coriander. Different cultures that grow coffee use it in different ways, and cooking with it is a wonderful way to experience the flavors of those cultures.

INGREDIENTS

SERVES 6

FOR THE ESPRESSO BBQ SAUCE
Makes 8 cups

4 cups ketchup

1 cup molasses

1 cup packed brown sugar

1 cup apple cider vinegar

1 cup freshly brewed espresso or coffee

Juice of 2 navel oranges (½ cup)

Juice of 2 lemons (¼ cup)

3 tablespoons Chef Kenny's Cinnamon Coffee Rub (to make your own, see page 16)

2 tablespoons Chef Kenny's Raging Cajun Spice, or other Cajun seasoning

2 tablespoons Chef Kenny's Fried Chicken Seasoning, or other poultry seasoning

1 tablespoon ground cumin

1 tablespoon kosher salt

1 teaspoon crushed red pepper

FOR THE RIBS

3 slabs St. Louis–style ribs

½ cup Chef Kenny's Cinnamon Coffee Rub (to make your own, see page 16)

3 cups Espresso BBQ Sauce (see above)

FOR THE SLAW

1 cup sour cream

½ cup agave nectar

Juice of 2 or 3 limes (¼ cup)

1 tablespoon kosher salt

1½ pounds green cabbage, grated (6 cups)

¼ large poblano pepper, finely diced (¼ cup)

¼ red onion, sliced (¼ cup)

¼ bunch cilantro, chopped (¼ cup)

¼ cup dill pickle relish

1 teaspoon Chef Kenny's Fried Chicken Seasoning, or other poultry seasoning

FOR THE BUILD

12 flour tortillas

Make the Espresso BBQ Sauce

1. In a medium saucepan over medium heat, whisk the ketchup, molasses, brown sugar, vinegar, espresso, orange and lemon juices, coffee rub, chicken seasoning, cumin, salt, and crushed red pepper. Bring to a simmer, then reduce the heat to low and cook for 15 minutes.

2. Remove from the heat and set aside until ready to use. (Any leftover sauce can be stored in an airtight container, in the refrigerator, for up to 6 months. It can be used as a substitute for any barbecue sauce.)

Make the Ribs

1. Preheat a smoker with charcoal and hickory wood to 275° or 300°F, or preheat an oven to 300°F.

2. Season the ribs on both sides with the coffee rub.

3. Set the ribs on the grate of the smoker, backbone side down, and cook for 1½ to 2 hours, or until the internal temperature is 165°F. Keep the smoker on. If cooking in the oven, put the ribs on sheet pans lined with foil and cook for 1½ to 2 hours, or until they reach an internal temperature of 165°F. Keep the oven on.

4. Transfer each of the slabs to a large sheet of foil, backbone side down. Pour 1 cup of the barbecue sauce over each slab and wrap them in the foil.

5. Return the ribs to the smoker or oven and cook for another 1¼ hours, or until they reach an internal temperature of 195°F.

6. Rest the foil-wrapped cooked ribs in a cooler (without ice) for a minimum of 30 minutes and a maximum of 3 hours before serving.

Make the Slaw

1. Whisk the sour cream, agave nectar, lime juice, and salt in a large bowl.

2. Add the cabbage, poblano, onion, cilantro, pickle relish, and chicken seasoning to the bowl and toss. Set aside until ready to serve.

The Build

1. Using a sharp chef's knife, cut the slabs of ribs into three-rib portions. Be sure to cut close to the bone of the next rib; that way every rib will have meat on the bone.

2. Heat a large cast-iron skillet on medium-high. Warm the tortillas on each side for 10 to 15 seconds, until lightly charred.

3. Place two griddled tortillas on a plate and top with three ribs. Add a small cup of barbecue sauce and some slaw. Plate the remaining servings, and serve additional slaw and barbecue sauce alongside.

Jerk-Spiced Spareribs with Coconut Guava Slaw

During the time of slavery in the Caribbean, enslaved people were often given scraps to eat that didn't have much meat, such as chitlins, offal, and ribs. Enslavers would take the meaty parts for themselves. Enslaved people learned how to cook tough pieces of meat over a fire until they were tender. They were resourceful enough to make them into something delicious. Pimento trees are indigenous to Jamaica, and they produce the allspice berry. The pimento wood enslaved people used in their firepits would smoke that allspice flavor into the meat. Allspice is the major component of jerk seasoning, which is so tied to the Caribbean. The bold flavors and colors of chiles such as Scotch bonnets and habaneros are a part of island culture. Removing the seeds from the chiles ensures a subtle heat that allows the fruity and complex spice of the peppers to shine (you will want to use kitchen gloves to do this), but if you want to maximize the heat of the spice do not remove the seeds. Throughout my life—from my childhood visits to the Caribbean to working there as an adult—I have had a deep love for the islands.

INGREDIENTS

SERVES 6

FOR THE HABANERO-MANGO BBQ SAUCE
Makes 7 cups

2 cups ketchup

2 cups yellow mustard

1 cup honey

1 cup coconut sugar

1 cup mango nectar

Juice of 2 lemons (¼ cup)

2 habanero peppers, finely chopped

2 Scotch bonnet peppers, finely chopped,
   or 1 tablespoon crushed red pepper

1 tablespoon kosher salt

FOR THE RIBS

3 slabs St. Louis–style ribs

½ cup Chef Kenny's Jerk Spice, or
   other jerk spice blend

3 cups Habanero-Mango BBQ Sauce
   (see above)

FOR THE SLAW

1 cup canned coconut milk, preferably
   Thai Kitchen

½ cup mayonnaise

½ cup guava paste

¼ cup coconut vinegar

Kosher salt

1½ pounds green cabbage, grated (6 cups)

½ medium red bell pepper, seeded and
   cut into small dice (½ cup)

1 teaspoon ground ginger

FOR THE BUILD

Mango wedges

**Make the
Habanero-Mango
BBQ Sauce**

1. Whisk the ketchup, mustard, honey, coconut sugar, mango nectar, lemon juice, habaneros, Scotch Bonnets, and salt in a medium saucepan. Bring to a simmer over medium heat. Reduce heat to low and cook for 15 minutes, stirring occasionally.

2. Remove from the heat and puree with a handheld stick blender until smooth. Set aside until ready to use. (Leftover sauce can be stored in an airtight container in the refrigerator.)

Make the Ribs

1. Preheat a smoker with charcoal and pecan wood to 275° or 300°F, or preheat the oven to 300°F.

2. Season the ribs on both sides with the jerk spice blend.

3. Set the ribs on the grate of the smoker, backbone side down, and cook for 1½ to 2 hours, or until the internal temperature is 165°F. Keep the smoker on. If cooking in the oven, put the ribs on sheet pans lined with foil and cook for 1½ to 2 hours, or until they reach an internal temperature of 165°F. Keep the oven on.

4. Transfer each of the slabs to a large sheet of foil, backbone side down. Pour 1 cup of the barbecue sauce over each slab and wrap them in the foil.

5. Return the ribs to the smoker or oven and cook for another 1¼ hours, or until they reach an internal temperature of 195°F.

6. Rest the foil-wrapped cooked ribs in a cooler (without ice) for a minimum of 30 minutes and a maximum of 3 hours before serving.

**Make the
Slaw and Sides**

In a large bowl, combine the coconut milk, mayonnaise, guava paste, vinegar, and salt with a handheld stick blender until smooth. Add the cabbage, bell pepper, and ginger and toss to combine.

The Build

1. Using a sharp chef's knife, cut the slabs of ribs into three-rib portions. Be sure to cut close to the bone of the next rib; that way every rib will have meat on the bone.

2. Put three ribs on a plate. Place barbecue sauce in a small cup on one side of the plate and some of the slaw on the other side. Garnish with a wedge of mango. Plate the remaining servings.

Wasabi, Honey, and Soy-Glazed Baby Back Ribs with Pineapple, Jicama, and Pickled Ginger Slaw

I grew up eating pork ribs in Ohio, which is traditional in the Midwestern United States as well as in the South. If I were from Texas, though, I'd probably have grown up eating beef ribs. Different parts of America have different rib styles and barbecue sauce preferences. Down in the Deep South, barbecue sauce tends to be sweeter, while in North Carolina it is vinegar based. Hawaii is an entirely different story when it comes to barbecue. Pork is the primary meat featured, and the barbecue sauce reflects the Asian immigrant influence on the culture there. The wasabi, honey, and soy glaze in this recipe were inspired by a sauce from a Hawaiian chef friend, who learned it from Asian Americans in Hawaii. There is a gentle balance between wasabi and soy flavors in this sauce, which is totally cravable. Pork is the best meat to allow these ingredients to shine.

FOR THE WASABI, HONEY, AND SOY GLAZE
Makes 4 cups

1 cup wasabi paste
2 cups honey
1 cup low-sodium soy sauce

FOR THE RIBS

¼ cup coconut sugar
3 tablespoons ground ginger
1 tablespoon ground turmeric
1 teaspoon freshly ground white pepper
Kosher salt
3 slabs St. Louis–style ribs
3 cups Wasabi, Honey, and Soy Glaze (see above)

FOR THE SLAW

½ cup mayonnaise
½ cup sour cream
½ cup honey
Juice of 2 or 3 limes (¼ cup)
1 tablespoon kosher salt
8 ounces napa cabbage, grated (2 cups)
5¾ ounces pineapple, cut into small dice (1 cup)
4½ ounces jicama, sliced (1 cup)
¼ medium red bell pepper, seeded and cut into small dice (¼ cup)
¼ medium red onion, chopped (¼ cup)
¼ bunch cilantro, chopped (¼ cup)
3 tablespoons chopped pickled ginger

FOR THE BUILD

3 limes, cut into wedges
1 pineapple, peeled, cored, and cut into wedges

Make the Wasabi, Honey, and Soy Glaze

Whisk the wasabi, honey, and soy sauce in a small saucepan and bring to a simmer over medium heat. Reduce the heat to low and cook for 15 minutes at a low simmer. Remove from the heat and set aside.

Make the Ribs

1. Preheat the oven to 300°F and line two sheet pans with foil.
2. Mix the coconut sugar, ginger, turmeric, white pepper, and salt to taste in a small bowl.
3. Season the ribs on both sides with the coconut sugar blend and place on the prepared sheet pans.
4. Cook the ribs for 1½ to 2 hours, or until they reach an internal temperature of 165°F. Remove the ribs but keep the oven on.
5. Transfer each of the slabs to a large sheet of foil, backbone side down. Pour 1 cup of the glaze over each slab and wrap them in the foil.
6. Return the ribs to the oven and cook for an additional 1¼ hours, or until they reach an internal temperature of 195°F.
7. Rest the foil-wrapped cooked ribs in a cooler (without ice) for a minimum of 30 minutes and a maximum of 3 hours before serving.

Make the Slaw

1. Whisk the mayonnaise, sour cream, honey, lime juice, and salt in a large bowl.
2. Add the cabbage, pineapple, jicama, bell pepper, onion, cilantro, and pickled ginger and toss to combine.

The Build

1. Preheat a grill to medium-high. Put the halved limes and pineapple wedges on the grill. Cook 3 to 5 minutes on each side, or until lightly charred.
2. Using a sharp chef's knife, cut the slabs of ribs into three-rib portions. Be sure to cut close to the bone of the next rib; that way every rib will have meat on the bone.
3. Place three ribs on a plate. Put some barbecue sauce in a small cup on the plate along with some of the slaw. Garnish with grilled lime and pineapple wedges. Repeat for the remaining servings.

BURGERS + FRIES

CARLOTTA'S EUCLID CREEK BURGER
WITH HAND-CUT STEAK FRIES

My mom's perfectly seasoned ground beef patty, grilled and served on
an onion kaiser roll with hand-cut steak fries and all the fixings

102

BLACK BEAN QUINOA BURGER WITH BABY ARTICHOKE
AND FINGERLING POTATO FRIES

California-vibes vegan and gluten-free burger served on
ciabatta bread with baby Tuscan kale, heirloom tomatoes,
and avocado, with a side of crispy baby artichoke
and fingerling potato fries and lemon aioli for dipping

106

THAI TURKEY BURGER WITH TEMPURA GREEN BEAN FRIES

Spicy and tangy Thai turkey burger served on a
sesame seed bun with green papaya slaw, butter lettuce,
and ginger-lime mayo, with a side of crispy tempura
green bean fries and nam prik caramel sauce

110

SMOKEHOUSE BURGER WITH SWEET POTATO FRIES

The best burger blend—beef brisket, beef chuck,
and smoked pork belly—cast-iron griddled, then topped with
smoked Gouda and mushroom-onion jam and served
on a pretzel bun with a heaping pile of sweet potato fries
and truffle-honey ketchup

114

Every American can relate to a burger. A great burger with a side of fries is a dish that resonates with our collective memories of childhood, cookouts, and life on the go. The burger is the iconic entrée of Labor Day, Memorial Day, and the Fourth of July. For me, burgers are about family time and vacation. They take me back to long summer days spent outside with my brother and friends. We would return home from playing in the creek behind our house to find my dad working the grill and Mom laying out a spread of burgers, hot dogs, and all the classic fixings: lettuce, tomato, onion, ketchup, yellow mustard, mayo, and buns. When I think of homemade burgers, I think of some of the happiest moments of my life.

We didn't know fast-food burgers growing up. I experienced fast food for the first time at the age of fifteen when I began my first job, at McDonald's. I started at the register, because I wasn't old enough to work in the kitchen. That didn't stop me, though. I would sneak back and work the grill, and I was good at it. Just before my sixteenth birthday, my boss told me I could work the burger board (what they called the grill). It was a system focused on efficiency and speed. On one side of the grill would be a pile of frozen burgers. I would drop the burgers on the grill to sear and then a beep would signal that it was time to season. Another beep would alert me that it was time to put the cheese on, and then one final beep was my cue to remove the patty. I could fly through cooking burgers on the burger board.

That's the thing about burgers: They are easy to make and are a complete meal all on their own—protein, carbohydrates, vegetables, and fruit (tomato). If you have a grill, you don't even have to dirty a pan to make a meal. In these recipes, the sauces, the fixings, and the burger meat itself can all be made a day ahead. When it's summertime, the grilling should be easy. Shoot, make it easy all the time. Life is too short.

Chef Skills: Burgers

I like to make my burger meat into a ball and roll it like a big meatball. Then I press it out in a ring mold to get it to a consistent ½-inch thickness. A burger will swell up when it cooks, because all its juices run to its center. If you press it down properly, there shouldn't be an issue. Some people put a dimple in the center to do this, but if you just flatten it out to ½ inch, it will work. Next, I sear the top and bottom of the burger on the hottest part of the grill or griddle. I don't touch it as it cooks. I just let it do its thing for 3 to 4 minutes per side. The key to a great burger is letting it cook and letting it rest.

Carlotta's Euclid Creek Burger with Hand-Cut Steak Fries

My mother, Carlotta, is the eldest of seven children. My grandmother was a diabetic, and she had to eat well-balanced meals with snacks in between throughout the day. My mother learned to cook out of necessity in order to care for her family, and she always brought bold flavor to the table. All I knew growing up was food that was well-seasoned, and my mom's burger recipe bursts with flavor. I grew up in Euclid, Ohio, and we celebrated summer holidays with cookouts. This burger reminds me of good times with family and friends.

Some people are burger purists and just use salt and pepper to season. This works great with a smash burger, which is a thinner patty seared on both sides. A thick, juicy burger needs to be seasoned throughout so every bite is flavorful . . . because every bite matters.

INGREDIENTS

SERVES 6

FOR THE STEAK FRIES

1 tablespoon Chef Kenny's Raging Cajun Spice,
  or other Cajun seasoning
1 teaspoon kosher salt
1 teaspoon granulated sugar
6 russet potatoes, scrubbed
4 cups peanut oil

FOR THE BURGER

2¼ pounds (70/30) ground beef
1 medium white or yellow onion, diced (1 cup)
1 medium green bell pepper, seeded and
  diced (1 cup)
4 ounces sharp cheddar cheese, grated (1 cup)
¼ cup Worcestershire sauce, preferably
  Lea & Perrins
¼ cup yellow mustard
1 tablespoon Lawry's Seasoned Salt
1 teaspoon freshly ground black pepper
1 teaspoon granulated garlic
12 slices American cheese

FOR THE BUILD

6 onion burger buns or kaiser rolls
  (plain or sesame)
Mayonnaise
Ketchup
Yellow mustard
6 pieces iceberg lettuce
6 (¼-inch-thick) slices red onion
6 (¼-inch-thick) slices tomato
12 dill pickle chips

Make the Steak Fries

1. Preheat the oven to 425°F.
2. Combine the Cajun seasoning, salt, and sugar in a small bowl, mixing well. Set aside.
3. Bake the potatoes on a sheet pan for about 1 hour, until easily pierced with a knife. Remove from the oven and reduce the oven temperature to 170°F. Allow the potatoes to cool to room temperature.
4. Once cool, cut the potatoes lengthwise into large wedges.
5. Heat the oil in a large Dutch oven on medium, or in a tabletop deep-fat fryer, and bring to 375°F.
6. Carefully place a small handful of potato wedges into the hot oil and fry for 2 minutes, or until golden brown. Use a long-handled strainer or spider to transfer the fries to a large bowl.
7. Season the fries with the Cajun seasoning mix while they are still hot. Continue with the remaining potatoes. Transfer to a sheet pan and keep warm in the oven.

Make the Burger

1. Preheat a charcoal or gas grill to medium-high heat. Or, if making on the stovetop, preheat a cast-iron skillet on medium-high for at least 5 minutes.
2. Combine the ground beef, onion, bell pepper, cheddar cheese, Worcestershire sauce, mustard, seasoned salt, black pepper, and granulated garlic in a large bowl, kneading gently with your hands until the ingredients are well incorporated.
3. Form 6 patties about ½ inch thick and place on a sheet pan.
4. Transfer the burgers to the grill or skillet and cook for 4 minutes per side for medium doneness, or until the desired doneness.
5. Top each burger with 2 slices of cheese and cover the grill or skillet for 1 minute, until the cheese has melted.

The Build

1. Line up the buns and add a generous tablespoon each of mayonnaise, ketchup, and mustard to the bottom buns.
2. Put a piece of lettuce, tomato, and onion on the bottom buns, then top with a cheesy burger patty. Put 2 dill pickle chips on top of each burger and finish with the top buns. Enjoy with the steak fries and ketchup.

Black Bean Quinoa Burger with Baby Artichoke and Fingerling Potato Fries

Texture and seasoning are the two things that can make or break a veggie burger. I love quinoa. It is high in protein, great for texture, and tastes delicious when seasoned. It pairs well with black beans, which add nice color and rich flavor to a veggie burger. The xanthan gum in this recipe binds the burger ingredients together. This recipe allows for a little flexibility, so try working in seasonal vegetables, like butternut squash in the fall. Experiment with it and have some fun.

SERVES 6

INGREDIENTS

FOR THE LEMON AIOLI
1 cup mayonnaise
Juice of 2 lemons (¼ cup)
1 tablespoon Dijon mustard
1 tablespoon garlic paste
1 teaspoon lemon pepper

FOR THE FRIES
12 fingerling potatoes or heirloom baby potatoes, halved lengthwise
4 cups grapeseed oil, or canola or corn oil
2 (14-ounce) cans quartered baby artichokes, drained and patted dry (2 cups)
2 cups potato starch
Kosher salt

FOR THE BURGER
¼ cup grapeseed oil
½ medium yellow onion, cut into small dice (½ cup)
1 medium carrot, diced (½ cup)
2 ribs celery, cut into small dice (½ cup)
½ cup chopped white button mushrooms
¼ cup chopped garlic (4 to 6 cloves)
1 cup cooked red quinoa (prepare according to package instructions)
2 (15-ounce) cans black beans, drained (3 cups)
1 bunch cilantro, leaves cut into thin ribbons (1 cup)
¼ cup potato starch
1 tablespoon kosher salt
¼ cup mild olive oil or vegetable oil

FOR THE BUILD
6 slices heirloom tomato
3 avocados, halved, pitted, and sliced
Kosher salt
6 ciabatta buns, halved and toasted
3 cups loosely packed baby Tuscan kale

Make the Lemon Aioli

Whisk the mayonnaise, lemon juice, mustard, garlic paste, and lemon pepper in a small bowl. Cover and refrigerate until ready to use.

Make the Fries

1. Preheat the oven to 425°F.
2. Put the potatoes on a sheet pan and bake for 20 minutes, or until easily pierced with a knife. Remove the potatoes and reduce the oven temperature to 170°F. Cool the potatoes to room temperature.
3. Heat the oil in a large Dutch oven on medium, or in a tabletop deep-fat fryer, and bring to 375°F.
4. In a large bowl, toss the potatoes and artichokes with the potato starch until fully coated.
5. Carefully put a small handful of potatoes and artichokes into the hot oil. Fry for about 2 minutes, until golden brown. Use a long-handled strainer or spider to transfer the potatoes and artichokes to a sheet pan; season with salt to taste and keep warm in the oven. Continue with the remaining potatoes and artichokes.

Make the Burgers

1. Preheat the oven to 425°F.
2. Heat a large cast-iron or nonstick skillet on medium for 1 minute, then coat with the grapeseed oil. Put the onion, carrot, celery, mushrooms, and garlic in the skillet and cook for 2 minutes, or until softened, stirring constantly.
3. Transfer the vegetables to a large bowl, then add the quinoa. Set aside. Clean the skillet.
4. Put the black beans in a food processor with metal blade and process for 1 minute, until pureed but still slightly chunky. Add the pureed black beans to the bowl with the vegetables and quinoa, then add the cilantro, potato starch, and salt. Mix with your hands until well combined. Form 6 patties ½ to ¾ inch thick and place on a plate.
5. Heat the skillet on medium-high. Coat the skillet with the olive oil, add the burgers, and sear for 1 to 2 minutes per side. You may need to do this in batches.
6. Once all the burgers are seared, transfer to a sheet pan and bake for 7 minutes.

The Build

1. Season the tomato and avocado with salt.
2. Spread some of the lemon aioli on a bottom bun. Layer kale and heirloom tomato on the bun. Place the burger on top of the tomato, then arrange avocado slices on the burger. Spread some of the aioli on the top bun and place it on the avocado. Plate the remaining servings. Enjoy with the artichoke and potato fries and the remaining aioli for dipping.

Thai Turkey Burger with Tempura Green Bean Fries

The Southeast Asian–inspired slaw on this burger is the key. Green papaya salad, or in this case slaw, typically has shrimp paste, raw sugar, fish sauce, basil, and tomatoes. It is bright and complex in taste and vibrant in color—and it takes this turkey burger to the next level.

SERVES 6

INGREDIENTS

FOR THE GREEN PAPAYA SLAW

½ cup halved cherry tomatoes
Juice of 2 or 3 limes (¼ cup)
¼ bunch Thai basil or sweet basil, leaves only (¼ cup)
2 Thai (bird) or serrano chiles, or jalapeño peppers, minced
2 tablespoons shrimp paste
1 tablespoon Sugar in The Raw
1 tablespoon fish sauce
1 teaspoon chopped garlic
1 green papaya, peeled, seeded, and thinly sliced (2 cups)
½ cup stemmed and sliced green beans
3 tablespoons roasted unsalted peanuts
Kosher salt

FOR THE GINGER-LIME MAYO

Makes 1½ cups

1 cup mayonnaise
¼ cup honey
Zest of 1 lime
Juice of 1 lime (2 tablespoons)
2 tablespoons ginger paste
Kosher salt

FOR THE NAM PRIK SAUCE

¼ cup water
1 cup granulated sugar
1 cup canned coconut milk
¼ cup fish sauce
Juice of 2 or 3 limes (¼ cup)
4 Thai (bird) or serrano chiles or jalapeño peppers, chopped
2 tablespoons chopped fresh cilantro

1 (1-inch) piece fresh ginger, peeled and minced (1 tablespoon)
1 tablespoon minced dried anchovies
1 tablespoon prepared Cambodian lemongrass paste or chopped fresh lemongrass
1 tablespoon shrimp paste
1 teaspoon Makrut lime powder
¼ teaspoon xanthan gum

FOR THE GREEN BEAN FRIES

4 cups peanut, canola, or corn oil
3 cups tempura flour
1 cup water
½ cup vodka
2 tablespoons ground ginger
2½ pounds green beans, stemmed
Kosher salt

FOR THE BURGER

3 pounds ground turkey
2 tablespoons fish sauce
¼ cup ginger paste
¼ cup prepared Cambodian lemongrass paste
¼ bunch cilantro, chopped (¼ cup)
1 tablespoon shrimp paste
2 Thai (bird) or serrano chiles, or jalapeño peppers, minced
1 tablespoon kosher salt
¾ cup duck fat or ghee

FOR THE BUILD

6 sesame seed burger buns, toasted
6 leaves butter lettuce
1 bunch cilantro, chopped (1 cup)
6 fresh Thai basil leaves, finely chopped
Lime wedges, for serving

**Make the
Green Papaya Slaw**

1. Put the cherry tomatoes, lime juice, Thai basil, chiles, shrimp paste, sugar, fish sauce, and garlic in a large bowl.
2. Mash up the ingredients with a wooden spoon or potato masher, gently crushing the tomatoes.
3. Add the papaya, green beans, peanuts, and salt to taste and toss together until combined. (The slaw can be made a few hours ahead and stored in the refrigerator.)

**Make the
Ginger-Lime Mayo**

Mix the mayonnaise, honey, lime zest, lime juice, ginger paste, and salt to taste in a small bowl. Set aside in the refrigerator until ready to use.

**Make the
Nam Prik Sauce**

1. Cook the water and sugar in a medium saucepan over medium-high heat, stirring to dissolve the sugar.
2. Continue stirring until the sugar caramelizes, about 15 minutes. It should turn an amber-brown color similar to honey.
3. Whisk in the coconut milk and bring to a boil, stirring constantly.
4. Add the fish sauce, lime juice, chiles, cilantro, fresh ginger, dried anchovies, lemongrass and shrimp pastes, lime powder, and xanthan gum and stir until the mixture thickens. Puree with a handheld stick blender until smooth. Remove from the heat and set aside.

Make the Fries

1. Heat the oil in a large Dutch oven on medium, or in a tabletop deep-fat fryer, and bring to 375°F. Line a sheet pan with paper towels.
2. Put 1½ cups of the tempura flour into a 1-gallon resealable plastic bag.
3. Mix the water, vodka, ground ginger, and remaining 1½ cups tempura flour in a medium bowl and transfer to another 1-gallon resealable plastic bag.
4. Put the green beans in the bag with the tempura flour, seal the bag, and shake to thoroughly dust.
5. Transfer the dusted green beans to the bag with the vodka-tempura batter. Coat thoroughly.
6. Carefully place a handful of the green beans in the hot oil and fry for 2 to 3 minutes, until golden brown. Use a long-handled strainer or spider to transfer the green beans to the prepared sheet pan. Season with salt and keep warm in a low (170°F) oven. Continue with the remaining green beans.

Make the Burger

1. Combine the turkey, fish sauce, ginger and lemongrass pastes, cilantro, shrimp paste, chiles, salt, and ½ cup of the duck fat in a large bowl, kneading gently with your hands until the ingredients are well incorporated.
2. Form 6 patties ½ to ¾ inch thick and place on a sheet pan.
3. Heat a large cast-iron or heavy-bottomed skillet on medium. Put the remaining ¼ cup duck fat in the skillet and heat for 1 minute, until melted.

4. Gently add the burgers to the skillet, in batches if necessary, and cook for 3 to 4 minutes on each side, until they reach a minimum of 165°F on an instant-read thermometer. Keep the burgers warm, on a sheet pan in the oven with the green bean fries.

The Build

1. Spread 1 tablespoon of the ginger-lime mayonnaise on the bottom half of each bun. Put a piece of the butter lettuce on each bottom bun and top with some of the green papaya slaw. Top the slaw with a burger. Sprinkle the burgers with cilantro and Thai basil leaves. Spread 1 tablespoon of the ginger-lime mayo on the top buns and place on the burgers.

2. Garnish each plate with a lime wedge, and enjoy with the green bean fries and nam prik sauce.

Smokehouse Burger with Sweet Potato Fries

American chefs love to create their own burgers, regardless of their personal cooking style, because of the nostalgia burgers bring and their popularity as menu items. This is my signature burger from my restaurant, Underground Kitchen, and guests loved it. The fat from the ground brisket, chuck, and smoked pork belly makes this so decadent and rich.

Pretzels are one of my favorite snacks, and I love a burger on a pretzel bun: the meat brings out the molasses flavor in the pretzel. Add the mushroom-onion jam, which is earthy and sweet, with the truffle-honey ketchup, which creates a beautiful marriage of acid and umami flavors, and you have an incredible burger that hits all the right flavor notes.

SERVES 6

FOR THE TRUFFLE-HONEY KETCHUP
Makes 3 cups

1 (28-ounce can) whole peeled tomatoes, tomatoes only (1 cup)

½ cup apple cider vinegar

½ cup honey

1 tablespoon black truffle oil

1 teaspoon kosher salt

¼ teaspoon crushed red pepper

FOR THE MUSHROOM-ONION JAM
Makes 4 cups

¼ cup extra-virgin olive oil

1 medium yellow or white onion, cut into small dice (1 cup)

6 ounces portobello mushrooms, coarsely diced (2 cups)

2 cloves garlic, chopped

1 cup apple cider vinegar

½ cup packed light brown sugar

2 or 3 sprigs rosemary, leaves only, chopped (¼ cup)

1 tablespoon freshly ground black pepper

1 teaspoon kosher salt

¼ teaspoon xanthan gum

FOR THE SWEET POTATO FRIES

2 tablespoons Chef Kenny's Cinnamon Coffee Rub (to make your own, see page 16)

1 tablespoon granulated sugar

1 tablespoon kosher salt

6 sweet potatoes

8 cups peanut, canola, or corn oil

FOR THE BURGER

1 pound ground beef brisket

1 pound ground beef chuck

4 ounces ground smoked pork belly, slab bacon, or bacon strips

¼ cup fried shallots, preferably Maesri

¼ cup fried garlic, preferably Maesri

¼ cup yellow mustard

2 tablespoons Chef Kenny's Fried Chicken Seasoning, or other poultry seasoning

FOR THE BUILD

Shredded smoked Gouda cheese

6 pretzel burger buns, toasted

**Make the
Truffle-Honey Ketchup**

1. Put the tomatoes, apple cider vinegar, honey, black truffle oil, salt, and crushed red pepper in a large saucepan and bring to a simmer on medium heat, stirring often.
2. Cook, uncovered, for 20 to 30 minutes, until the liquid in the pan has reduced by half. Puree the mixture with a handheld stick blender until smooth.
3. Cool and reserve at room temperature until ready to use. (Any remaining ketchup can be stored in an airtight container in the refrigerator.)

**Make the
Mushroom-Onion Jam**

1. Heat a medium skillet on medium-high. Add the olive oil and the onions and cook for 1 minute, stirring constantly.
2. Add the mushrooms and cook for 2 minutes, stirring constantly. Reduce the heat to medium and add the garlic, apple cider vinegar, brown sugar, rosemary, pepper, salt, and xanthan gum.
3. Cook for 10 minutes, until the vegetables are tender and the consistency is jammy. Remove from the heat and reserve at room temperature until ready to use. (Any leftovers can be stored in an airtight container in the refrigerator. It can be served with grilled steak or chicken, or with Brie or similar cheeses.)

**Make the
Sweet Potato Fries**

1. Preheat the oven to 425°F.
2. Combine the cinnamon coffee rub, sugar, and salt in a small bowl, mixing well. Set aside.
3. Wash and dry the sweet potatoes and cut into finger-sized strips. Place the strips on a sheet pan.
4. Bake the potatoes for 20 minutes, or until easily pierced with a knife. Remove from the oven and reduce the oven temperature to 170°F. Allow the potatoes to cool to room temperature.
5. Heat the oil in a large Dutch oven on medium, or in a tabletop deep-fat fryer, and bring to 375°F.
6. Carefully place a small handful of potaotes in the hot oil. Fry in small batches for 2 minutes, or until golden brown. Use a long-handled strainer or spider to transfer the fries to a large bowl. Season with the spice mixture to taste. Keep warm on a sheet pan in the oven. Continue with the remaining potatoes.

Make the Burger

1. Preheat a charcoal or gas grill to medium-high, or heat a cast-iron or other heavy-bottomed skillet on medium-high.
2. Combine the ground brisket, chuck, and pork belly in a large bowl, gently mixing with your hands.
3. Add the fried shallots, fried garlic, yellow mustard, and chicken seasoning to the bowl and gently mix with your hands until the ingredients are well incorporated.
4. Form 6 patties about ½ inch thick and place on a sheet pan.
5. Transfer the burgers to the grill or skillet and cook for 2 to 4 minutes per side for medium doneness, or until the desired doneness.

The Build

1. Place a pile of shredded Gouda cheese on each burger, then place back on the grill until the cheese has melted. Alternatively, put the burgers on a sheet pan, add the cheese, and broil until the cheese has melted. Remove the fries before turning on the broiler.

2. Spread 1 tablespoon of the truffle-honey ketchup on the bottom and top halves of each bun. Place the burgers on top of the bottom buns. Add some of the mushroom-onion jam to each burger and finish with the top buns.

3. Enjoy with the sweet potato fries and any remaining ketchup.

OXTAILS
+ RICE

DEEP SOUTH OXTAILS WITH BUTTERY WHITE RICE

Slowly braised oxtails in a delicious brown gravy with tender roasted root vegetables, served over buttery white rice and steamed cabbage

124

FILIPINO OXTAIL ADOBO WITH
GARLIC RICE AND RED QUINOA

Beef oxtails braised in a tangy soy-vinegar broth, spiced with black peppercorns, bay leaves, garlic, and crushed red pepper, and served over a mixture of garlicky brown jasmine rice and red quinoa with baby bok choy

128

GUYANESE OXTAIL PEPPER POT WITH RICE FRITTERS

Peppery braised oxtails with cassareep, bell peppers, habaneros, and root vegetables, served with rice fritters and roasted cabbage

132

CLAY POT–STEAMED OXTAILS WITH CONGEE

Chinese-style steamed oxtails with ginseng root, served with congee and topped with classic congee garnishes

136

CHIANTI-BRAISED OXTAILS WITH
PORCINI MUSHROOM RISOTTO

Chianti-braised oxtails with hints of rosemary and garlic, served on porcini mushroom risotto and salsa verde

140

Soul food is a cuisine named for the style of cooking of enslaved people in the American South. On plantations throughout the South and in the Caribbean, enslaved people had nothing to eat other than what they grew or foraged themselves, or what was given to them by plantation owners. Like baby back ribs, oxtails were considered a scrap meat by the plantation owners. While I grew up eating many traditional soul food dishes, oxtails were not a dish I tried until I was older.

The first time I had oxtails was at a Jamaican restaurant in Florida. It is a staple in Jamaican cuisine. Smothered in a brown gravy and served over rice, oxtails are a rich comfort food. When I worked at the Ritz-Carlton, Amelia Island, we would use them to stuff ravioli and in many other ways, elevating them for fine dining.

Oxtails are the tail of a cow. Their soul food–style preparation has its roots in the one-pot cooking of enslaved Africans. It takes a lot of cooking to tenderize the muscle fibers in the meat: first the oxtail is roasted, then it is braised for at least three hours. Many cultures across the world have their own way of preparing oxtails. As I created these recipes, I thought of the many immigrants who live in America. I reflected on the traditional foods that they love and thought of ways to adapt this delicious iconic dish of the American South so anyone can enjoy it within the context of their own unique American experience.

Oxtails

Oxtails can be found at your local butcher, ethnic market, or grocery store. They are usually sold in 2- to 3-inch-thick pieces. When you cook oxtails, they render a lot of fat that can be used in other recipes, like the drop biscuits in the Chicken + Biscuits chapter, page 20. Just replace ¼ cup melted butter in the recipe with ¼ cup oxtail fat. It will add a new level of richness in flavor to the biscuit.

Deep South Oxtails with Buttery White Rice

This is your classic soul food preparation of oxtails. It has a great savory flavor thanks to the meat and the bay leaves. Bay leaves create an earthy flavor that perfumes the braising broth nicely. The cabbage stands up well to the richness of the meat, and the white rice serves as a blank canvas for the gravy. It is comfort food at its best.

SERVES 6

FOR THE OXTAILS

2 cups canola oil
¼ cup Chef Kenny's Fried Chicken Seasoning,
    or other poultry seasoning
¼ cup Chef Kenny's Raging Cajun Spice,
    or other Cajun seasoning
2 tablespoons kosher salt
3 pounds oxtails
10 cups low-sodium beef stock
2 cups canned diced tomatoes (about two-thirds
    of a 28-ounce can)
1 cup Worcestershire sauce, preferably
    Lea & Perrins
6 bay leaves
2 teaspoons xanthan gum
2 medium yellow or white onions, cut into large
    dice (2 cups)
10 ounces carrots, cut into large dice (2 cups)
8 ribs celery, cut into large dice (2 cups)
10 cloves garlic, peeled

FOR THE RICE

4 cups low-sodium vegetable stock
2 cups long-grain white rice
½ cup (1 stick) salted butter
1 tablespoon kosher salt

FOR THE CABBAGE

½ cup (1 stick) salted butter
1 Spanish onion, cut into large dice
2 tablespoons chopped garlic
2 bay leaves
2 cups low-sodium vegetable stock
1 medium head green cabbage, cut into large dice
Kosher salt and freshly ground black pepper

FOR THE BUILD

Fresh sage leaves, for garnish

Make the Oxtails

1. Preheat the oven to 425°F.
2. Whisk the oil, chicken and Cajun seasonings, and salt in a small bowl.
3. Put the oxtails in a large bowl and add half the seasoned oil; set aside the remaining oil. Toss until the oxtails are well coated.
4. Transfer the oxtails with the seasoned oil to a large, deep casserole or Dutch oven that can accommodate the oxtails in one or two layers. Roast for 30 minutes, uncovered.
5. Combine the stock, chopped tomatoes with their juices, Worcestershire sauce, and bay leaves in a large pot and bring to a boil over high heat. Reduce the heat to medium and cook for 10 minutes. Remove and discard the bay leaves.
6. Add the xanthan gum to the stock mixture and puree with a handheld stick blender until smooth. Keep warm over low heat.
7. Place the onions, carrots, celery, and garlic in a large bowl and toss with the remaining seasoned oil.
8. Add the vegetables and their oil to the oxtails and roast, uncovered, for another 30 minutes.
9. Reduce the oven temperature to 350°F. Remove the oxtails from the oven. Pour the stock mixture over the oxtails to cover. (Any remaining stock mixture can be cooled and poured into a freezer-safe airtight container and frozen for later use.)
10. Cover the oxtail dish with a lid or parchment paper topped with a sheet of foil. Return the oxtails to the oven and braise for 2½ hours, until the meat is fork-tender.
11. Remove from the oven. Skim the fat that has risen to the top and either discard or save it (see box, page 123).

Make the Rice

1. Pour the stock into a large saucepan and bring to a boil over high heat.
2. Rinse the rice in a large bowl with cold water until the water runs clear. Drain through a fine-mesh sieve.
3. Add the rice to the boiling stock. Bring back to a boil and stir.
4. Reduce the heat to a simmer and cover the pot. Cook for 20 minutes, until the water is absorbed and the rice is tender but not mushy.
5. Remove the lid and add the butter and salt, stirring gently with a fork or wooden spoon. Cover with the lid to keep warm.

Make the Cabbage

1. Place the butter, onion, garlic, bay leaves, and stock in a large pot. Bring to a boil over high heat.
2. Add the cabbage and reduce the heat to medium-low. Cover and cook for 30 minutes, stirring occasionally.
3. When the cabbage is fork-tender, season with salt and pepper to taste.

The Build

1. Put rice into the center of six large bowls and add 2 oxtails to each bowl.
2. Add some of the cabbage and some of the root vegetables that cooked with the oxtails to each bowl, smother them with oxtail gravy, and garnish with sage leaves.

Filipino Oxtail Adobo with Garlic Rice and Red Quinoa

You meet all kinds of people from all parts of the world working in kitchens. One of my best friends is a Filipino chef name Rey. He introduced me to adobo while we were working together. He made chicken adobe for a staff meal one day, and it was amazing. The soy, vinegar, garlic, bay leaves, calamansi juice, and peppercorns in adobo create a unique acidic, savory taste in this classic Filipino dish. Calamansi is a citrus fruit found in the Philippines. It resembles a key lime, but tastes like a combination of orange, lemon, and lime. The complexity of its flavor is great for cooking. Bottled calamansi juice can be found online if it's not available at a local market.

SERVES 6

FOR THE OXTAILS
2 cups canola oil
¼ cup ground black pepper
1 tablespoon kosher salt
3 pounds oxtails
8 cups low-sodium beef stock
1 cup tamari
1 cup coconut vinegar
½ cup bottled calamansi juice
1 teaspoon crushed red pepper
12 bay leaves
2 teaspoons xanthan gum
3 medium yellow or white onions, diced (3 cups)
½ cup sliced fresh ginger
15 cloves garlic (1 cup)

FOR THE RICE AND QUINOA
¼ cup sesame oil
1 cup brown jasmine rice
10 cups (2½ quarts) water
Kosher salt
1 cup red quinoa
½ cup fried garlic, preferably Maesri
¼ cup fried shallots, preferably Maesri
1 tablespoon Chef Kenny's Fried Chicken Seasoning, or other poultry seasoning
½ cup tamari

FOR THE BOK CHOY
Kosher salt
3 baby bok choy, leaves separated

FOR THE BUILD
Fried shallots, preferably Maesri
Fried garlic, preferably Maesri
1 bunch cilantro, leaves only (1 cup)
Serrano chiles, sliced
Radishes, quartered and stored in ice water

Make the Oxtails

1. Preheat the oven to 425°F.
2. Whisk the oil, black pepper, and salt in a small bowl.
3. Put the oxtails in a large bowl and add half the seasoned oil; set aside the remaining oil. Toss until the oxtails are well coated.
4. Transfer the oxtails with the seasoned oil to a large, deep casserole or Dutch oven that can accommodate the oxtails in one or two layers. Roast for 30 minutes, uncovered.
5. Combine the stock, tamari, coconut vinegar, calamansi juice, crushed red pepper, and bay leaves in a large pot and bring to a boil over high heat. Reduce the heat to medium and cook for 10 minutes. Remove the bay leaves and discard.
6. Add the xanthan gum to the stock mixture and puree with a handheld stick blender until smooth. Keep warm over low heat.
7. Put the onions, ginger, and garlic in a medium bowl and toss with the remaining seasoned oil.
8. Add the vegetables and their oil to the oxtails and roast, uncovered, for another 30 minutes.
9. Reduce the oven temperature to 350°F. Remove the oxtails from the oven. Pour the stock mixture over the oxtails to cover. (Any remaining stock mixture can be cooled and poured into a freezer-safe airtight container and frozen for later use.)
10. Cover the oxtail dish with a lid or parchment paper topped with a sheet of foil. Return the oxtails to the oven and braise for 2½ hours, until the meat is fork-tender.
11. Remove from the oven. Skim the fat that has risen to the top and either discard or save it (see box, page 123).

Make the Rice and Quinoa

1. Pour the sesame oil into a large saucepan and heat on low.
2. Rinse the rice in a large bowl with cold water until the water runs clear. Drain in a fine-mesh sieve.
3. Add the rice to the sesame oil and stir until the rice is completely coated in the oil.
4. Add 2 cups water and bring to a boil. Reduce the heat to a simmer, cover, and cook for 20 minutes, until the water is absorbed and the rice is tender but not mushy. Once cooked, remove the cover and add salt to taste. Stir gently with a fork or wooden spoon and cover to keep warm.
5. Meanwhile, put 8 cups (2 quarts) water in a large pot and bring to a boil. Add the quinoa and cook for 8 minutes, or until the quinoa grains crack and open.
6. Drain the quinoa through a fine-mesh strainer and rinse with cool water to remove excess starch.
7. Put the rice and quinoa in a large bowl and toss to combine. Add the fried garlic, fried shallots, chicken seasoning, and tamari and stir until thoroughly combined. Cover the bowl with foil to keep warm until ready to serve.

Make the Bok Choy

Just before serving, bring a large pot of lightly salted water to a boil. Add the bok choy leaves and blanch for 45 seconds, then drain.

The Build

1. Put the rice and quinoa into the center of six large plates and top with 2 oxtails per plate. Add some of the steamed baby bok choy.
2. Spoon the oxtail braising juices over the oxtails, rice, and baby bok choy, and garnish with fried shallots, fried garlic, cilantro, chiles, and radishes.

Guyanese Oxtail Pepper Pot with Rice Fritters

I learned how to make the Guyanese pepper pot while living in Barbados. Both Barbados and Guyana were territories of Great Britain, and today many Guyanese live in Barbados. Pepper pot is a celebratory meal made for the holidays using leftover meat scraps, cassareep—an extract made from cassava—and a chunk of cassava. A pepper pot is not a pepper pot without cassareep. To make cassareep, the cassava is harvested and crushed in the same mills as sugarcane, then it is cooked down with nutmeg, cinnamon, cloves, and chiles. It becomes an extract that looks a lot like molasses and is full of complex flavor.

INGREDIENTS

SERVES 6

FOR THE OXTAILS
2 cups canola oil
¼ cup Chef Kenny's Cinnamon Coffee Rub (to make your own, see page 16)
¼ cup Chef Kenny's Jerk Spice, or other jerk seasoning
1 tablespoon kosher salt
3 pounds oxtails
10 cups low-sodium beef stock
1 cup canned diced tomatoes
1 cup cassareep, preferably Real Guyana Original Pomeroon Cassareep
6 star anise pods
1 fresh habanero pepper, chopped
1 medium yellow or white onion, cut into large dice (1 cup)
5 ounces carrots, cut into large dice (1 cup)
4 medium ribs celery, cut into large dice (1 cup)
1 medium red bell pepper, seeded and cut into large dice (1 cup)
10 cloves garlic, peeled

FOR THE RICE FRITTERS
4 cups canola oil
2 large eggs
1 medium rib celery, cut into large dice (¼ cup)
½ small Spanish white onion, cut into large dice (¼ cup)
¼ red bell pepper, stemmed and seeded, cut into large dice (¼ cup)
5 cloves garlic, peeled
½ cup buttermilk
2½ cups self-rising flour
1 cup cooked long-grain white rice, preferably Uncle Ben's
¼ bunch flat-leaf parsley, leaves chopped (¼ cup)
Kosher salt
4 tablespoons (½ stick) salted butter, melted

FOR THE CABBAGE
1 cup canola oil
2 tablespoons ground ginger
2 tablespoons granulated sugar
1 tablespoon kosher salt
½ teaspoon freshly ground black pepper
1 medium head green cabbage, cut into 6 or more large wedges

FOR THE BUILD
Fresh marjoram or oregano leaves
Sliced Fresno chiles

Make the Oxtails

1. Preheat the oven to 425°F.
2. Whisk the oil, cinnamon coffee and jerk seasonings, and salt in a small bowl.
3. Put the oxtails in a large bowl and add half the seasoned oil; set aside the remaining oil. Toss until the oxtails are well coated.
4. Transfer the oxtails and their seasoned oil to a large, deep casserole or Dutch oven that can accommodate the oxtails in one or two layers. Roast for 30 minutes, uncovered.
5. Combine the stock, diced tomatoes, cassareep, star anise, and habanero in a large pot and bring to a boil over high heat. Reduce the heat to medium and cook for 30 minutes. Remove the star anise and discard. Keep warm over low heat.
6. Place the onion, carrots, celery, bell pepper, and garlic in a large bowl and toss with the remaining seasoned oil.
7. Add the vegetables and their oil to the oxtails and roast, uncovered, for another 10 minutes.
8. Reduce the oven temperature to 350°F. Remove the oxtails from the oven. Pour the hot stock mixture over the oxtails to cover. (Any remaining stock mixture can be cooled and poured into a freezer-safe airtight container and frozen for later use.)
9. Cover the oxtail dish with a lid or parchment paper topped with a sheet of foil. Return the oxtails to the oven and braise for 2½ hours, until the meat is fork-tender.
10. Remove from the oven. Skim the fat that has risen to the top and either discard or save it (see box, page 123).

Make the Rice Fritters

1. Pour the canola oil into a large saucpean or tabletop deep-fat fryer and bring the oil to a temperature of 350°F. Line a sheet pan with paper towels.
2. To a blender, add the eggs, celery, onion, bell pepper, garlic, and buttermilk and blend until smooth.
3. Place the flour, rice, parsley, and some salt in a large bowl. Add the egg-vegetable mixture and the melted butter. Mix thoroughly until a batter forms.
4. Use a small scoop or spoon to gently place some of the rice batter into the hot oil (you will need to do this in batches). Fry the fritters for 1½ to 2 minutes, or until golden brown. Remove the fritters with a long-handled strainer or spider and drain on the prepared sheet pan. Continue with the remaining batter (the batter makes about 30 small fritters).

Make the Roasted Cabbage

1. Preheat the broiler and line a sheet pan with foil.
2. Whisk the oil, ginger, sugar, salt, and pepper in a large bowl.
3. Add the cabbage wedges to the bowl and toss gently in the spiced oil mixture.
4. Place the cabbage on the prepared sheet pan and broil for 5 minutes on the middle rack of the oven. Flip the cabbage and broil the other side for another 5 minutes.

The Build

1. Place a wedge of roasted cabbage in a bowl. Put 2 oxtails to the side of the cabbage along with some of the vegetables from the oxtails. Spoon oxtail braising juices over the oxtails and vegetables.

2. Set a few rice fritters around the oxtails and garnish with fresh marjoram or oregano leaves and sliced chiles. Plate the remaining servings.

Clay Pot–Steamed Oxtails with Congee

When I was working at the Ritz-Carlton in Osaka, Japan, a guest came in with some fresh ginseng root he had grown himself. He asked the chef to cook Silkie chicken soup, which is a brothy dish made from a special type of chicken called a Silkie, which has black skin. It is cooked in a clay pot, which seals in all the flavors, creating a phenomenally fragrant dish. Asian markets carry clay pots, but cooking this dish—inspired by the Silkie chicken soup—works in a Dutch oven, too. No matter what you cook it in, when you smell the oxtails cooking in this preparation, you will be blown away.

SERVES 6

FOR THE OXTAILS
10 cups low-sodium beef stock
6 pounds oxtails
3 medium yellow or white onions, cut into
    large dice (3 cups)
2 cups tamari
1 cup water
1 cup sliced fresh ginger
1 cup peeled garlic cloves (about 15 cloves)
4 tablespoons instant ginseng root tea granules
1 tablespoon kosher salt
1 tablespoon freshly ground black pepper

FOR THE CONGEE
1 cup sticky rice
5 cups water or vegetable stock

FOR THE BOK CHOY
Kosher salt
3 baby bok choy, leaves separated

FOR THE BUILD
3 scallions, sliced (1 cup) and stored in
    ice water until needed
1 bunch cilantro, leaves only (1 cup)
½ cup sliced red radishes (about 4)
½ cup fried shallots, preferably Maesri
¼ cup fried garlic, preferably Maesri
¼ cup sliced serrano chiles
2 tablespoons benne or sesame seeds

Make the Oxtails

1. Preheat the oven to 425°F.
2. To a large clay pot or Dutch oven add the stock, oxtails, onions, tamari, water, ginger, garlic, tea granules, salt, and pepper.
3. Braise, covered, for 2¾ hours, until the meat is fork-tender. Allow the oxtails to cool to room temperature, then pick the meat off the bones and reserve.
4. Strain the braising juices through a fine-mesh sieve into another pot. Bring the braising juices to a boil on high heat. Lower the heat to medium and simmer, uncovered, until the juices are reduced by half.
5. Add the picked meat to the braising sauce, and keep warm on low heat until ready to serve.

Make the Congee

Cook the rice and water in a large pot over medium heat for 30 to 40 minutes, until the rice is the consistency of porridge. Stir occasionally to keep the rice from sticking to the bottom of the pot.

Make the Bok Choy

Bring a large pot of lightly salted water to a boil. Add the baby bok choy leaves and blanch for 45 seconds. Drain and transfer the leaves to a bowl.

The Build

Place some of the congee in the center of a bowl. Top with a helping of the picked oxtail meat (more of the meat than braising sauce). Put bok choy and toppings around the oxtail meat in separate piles. Plate the remaining servings.

Chianti-Braised Oxtails with Porcini Mushroom Risotto

I love osso buco. I have cooked it more times than I can count, and it is the inspiration for this recipe. The mushroom risotto is earthy and creamy, and really complements the oxtails. It is easier to find dried porcini mushrooms than fresh, and they are less expensive. To me, whether dried or fresh, porcinis have the best flavor of any mushroom out there. The cabbage salsa verde completes the dish and brings in a Mexican element as well.

SERVES 6

INGREDIENTS

FOR THE OXTAILS

2 cups canola oil

½ cup dried porcini mushroom powder, preferably Orgnisulmte Organic

1 tablespoon kosher salt

6 pounds oxtails

8 cups low-sodium beef stock

2 cups canned diced tomatoes (about two-thirds of a 28-ounce can)

½ cup rehydrated porcini mushrooms, preferably Vigorous Mountains

1 (750-ml) bottle Chianti

½ bunch rosemary, leaves only, chopped (½ cup)

6 bay leaves

1 tablespoon xanthan gum

1 medium yellow or white onion, cut into large dice (1 cup)

5 ounces carrots, cut into large dice (1 cup)

4 medium ribs celery, cut into large dice (1 cup)

10 cloves garlic, peeled

FOR THE RISOTTO

½ cup Better Than Bouillon Mushroom Base

8 cups water

½ cup extra-virgin olive oil

2 small Spanish onions, cut into small dice (1 cup)

1 cup rehydrated porcini mushrooms, chopped, preferably Vigorous Mountains

2 tablespoons chopped garlic

2 cups arborio rice

½ cup (1 stick) salted butter

½ cup mascarpone cheese

¼ cup grated Parmesan cheese

Kosher salt and freshly ground black pepper

FOR THE SALSA VERDE

4 ounces green cabbage, finely chopped (1 cup)

½ medium red onion, cut into small dice (½ cup)

½ bunch flat-leaf parsley, leaves chopped (½ cup)

½ cup extra-virgin olive oil

2 to 3 sprigs rosemary, leaves only, chopped (¼ cup)

¼ bunch basil, leaves only, cut into ribbons (¼ cup)

8 dried, brined, or salt-cured anchovies, chopped

5 cloves garlic, thinly sliced

2 jalapeño peppers, finely chopped

Zest and juice of 1 lemon (about 2 tablespoons juice)

1 teaspoon Espelette pepper

Pinch of kosher salt

Make the Oxtails

1. Preheat the oven to 425°F.
2. Whisk the oil, porcini mushroom powder, and salt in a small bowl.
3. Put the oxtails in a large bowl and add half the seasoned oil; set aside the remaining oil. Toss until the oxtails are well coated.
4. Transfer the oxtails and their seasoned oil to a large, deep casserole or Dutch oven that can accommodate the oxtails in one or two layers. Roast for 30 minutes, uncovered.
5. Combine the stock, diced tomatoes, rehydrated porcini mushrooms, Chianti, rosemary, and bay leaves in a large pot and bring to a boil over high heat. Reduce the heat to medium and cook for 30 minutes. Remove the bay leaves and discard.
6. Add the xanthan gum to the stock mixture and puree with a handheld stick blender. Keep warm over low heat.
7. Place the onion, carrots, celery, and garlic into a large bowl and toss with the remaining seasoned oil.
8. Add the vegetables and their owl to the oxtails and roast, uncovered, for another 10 minutes.
9. Reduce the oven temperature to 350°F. Remove the oxtails from the oven. Pour the hot stock mixture over the oxtails to cover. (Any remaining stock mixture can be cooled and poured into a freezer-safe airtight container and frozen for later use.)
10. Cover the oxtail dish with a lid or parchment paper topped with a sheet of foil.
11. Place the oxtails back in the oven and braise for 2½ hours, until the meat is fork-tender.
12. Remove from the oven. Skim the fat that has risen to the top and either discard or save it (see box, page 123). Pick the oxtail meat from the bones and reserve.

Make the Risotto

1. Put the mushroom base and water in a medium saucepan over high heat. Stir to dissolve the bouillon and bring to a boil. Once boiling, reduce the heat to a simmer.
2. Warm a large rondeau pan or large shallow pot on medium heat. Add the olive oil, onions, rehydrated mushrooms, and garlic. Cook, stirring constantly, until the vegetables begin to soften.
3. Add the rice, stirring to thoroughly coat the rice kernels.
4. Add 1 cup of the mushroom stock to the rice mixture and cook, stirring constantly, until the rice absorbs the stock. Repeat this step until all the stock is added. The rice will release its starch and the risotto will take on a loose, creamy texture.
5. Add the butter, mascarpone cheese, Parmesan, and salt and pepper to taste, and stir gently to combine. Remove from the heat and cover to keep warm until ready to serve.

Make the Salsa Verde

In a large bowl, toss the cabbage, onion, parsley, olive oil, rosemary, basil, anchovies, garlic, jalapeños, lemon zest and juice, Espelette pepper, and salt to thoroughly combine.

The Build

1. Put risotto in the center of a bowl. Place some of the oxtail meat in the bowl, nestling it in the risotto.
2. Add some of the vegetables to the bowl and spoon the sauce over the vegetables, risotto, and oxtail meat. Garnish with some of the salsa verde. Plate the remaining servings.

CHICKEN + MAC & CHEESE

GILBERT'S BBQ CHICKEN WITH ANNA'S MAC & CHEESE

Smoky barbecue chicken legs seasoned with Raging Cajun spices
and glazed with barbecue sauce, served with my wife Anna's
mac & cheese—a shell pasta with black pepper cheese sauce and pimento
cheese with a sharp cheddar and Monterey Jack cheese gratin

150

LEMON AND ROSEMARY ROASTED CHICKEN BREASTS
WITH TALEGGIO-PANCETTA MAC & CHEESE

Roasted rosemary and garlic chicken breasts served with
Taleggio-pancetta mac & cheese with toasted rosemary breadcrumbs

154

CHICKEN WING MOLE WITH
CHARRED CORN–JALAPEÑO MAC & CHEESE

Braised chicken wings in black bean mole sauce served with
farfalle pasta and charred corn–jalapeño queso

158

BULGOGI-STYLE GRILLED CHICKEN THIGHS WITH
ASPARAGUS-SPINACH MAC & CHEESE

Bulgogi-marinated chicken thighs grilled with rigatoni pasta and
fried garlic cheese sauce served with asparagus and spinach

162

PORT-GLAZED CHICKEN THIGHS WITH
SAINT ANDRÉ–WHITE TRUFFLE MAC & CHEESE

Port-glazed roasted chicken thighs served with cavatappi pasta laced with Saint
André Mornay sauce and accented with white truffle oil, fennel, and shallot

166

Mac & cheese is a very relatable, homey dish. It is a meal that is a reminder of childhood for many Americans. My fondest memories of this dish are from family get-togethers. My mom made a great baked mac & cheese, almost like a macaroni pie, with many different cheeses, diced bell peppers, celery, and onion. In Black culture, baked macaroni always makes an appearance at family gatherings. Different families have their own recipes, but the style of cooking is the same—a variety of cheeses tossed with cooked pasta and baked in a casserole or pan until all the cheese is melted into the pasta and the top is browned.

All kids growing up in America, regardless of their cultural background, are going to eat mac & cheese at some point. We always had the iconic blue boxes of mac & cheese in our pantry when I was a kid. It was so bad but so good at the same time. I was six years old when I made my first box. I would doctor it up by adding more cheese to make it as cheesy as possible. I thought I was a big shot standing at the stove cooking "my own recipe."

I have cooked many different variations of mac & cheese over the years. Chicken is a great lean meat to serve with mac & cheese, and the added protein makes for a complete meal. I feel like pasta with any kind of cheese sauce is a version of mac & cheese—fettuccine Alfredo, for example. It is a classic comfort food, and entirely cravable. There is no better combination than cooked noodles with a rich and creamy sauce. Here I have created a series of recipes that explore this iconic American dish within the flavors of the world cultures that make up the United States.

CHICKEN + MAC & CHEESE

Gilbert's BBQ Chicken with Anna's Mac & Cheese

When my wife, Anna, and I opened our first restaurant together, Gilbert's Underground Kitchen, we knew we had to have mac & cheese on the menu. People loved it, but Anna always felt it was missing something. One day I watched her make her mac & cheese. She added a cheese combination similar to my pimento cheese—and a new variation was born.

SERVES 6

FOR THE BBQ SAUCE
Makes 4 cups

2 cups ketchup
½ cup apple cider vinegar
½ cup molasses
Juice of 3 lemons (¼ cup)
Juice of 1 navel orange (¼ cup)
¼ cup packed light brown sugar
2 tablespoons Chef Kenny's Raging Cajun Spice, or other Cajun seasoning
1 tablespoon Chef Kenny's Fried Chicken Seasoning, or other poultry seasoning
1 tablespoon ground cinnamon
¼ teaspoon kosher salt

FOR THE BBQ CHICKEN
½ cup corn oil
¼ cup Chef Kenny's Fried Chicken Seasoning, or other poultry seasoning
¼ cup Chef Kenny's Raging Cajun Spice, or other Cajun seasoning
Juice of 2 lemons
2 tablespoons kosher salt
12 jumbo chicken legs
1 cup BBQ Sauce (see above)

FOR THE MAC & CHEESE

For the Black Pepper Cheese Sauce
Makes 6 cups

3 cups half-and-half
1 cup lager
2 tablespoons freshly ground black pepper
1 tablespoon kosher salt
½ cup fried shallots, preferably Maesri
½ cup fried garlic, preferably Maesri

4 ounces (½ block) cream cheese
2 ounces Colby Jack cheese, shredded (½ cup)
2 ounces Monterey Jack cheese, shredded (½ cup)
2 ounces pepper Jack cheese, shredded (½ cup)
2 ounces sharp Cheddar cheese, shredded (½ cup)
¼ teaspoon xanthan gum

For the Pimento Cheese
Makes 2½ cups

½ cup cottage cheese
4 ounces (½ block) cream cheese
2 ounces sharp Cheddar cheese, shredded (½ cup)
2 ounces Monterey Jack cheese, shredded (½ cup)
¼ cup sour cream
¼ cup Chef Kenny's South Carolina Mustard BBQ Sauce or Sweet Baby Ray's Golden Mustard Barbecue Sauce
2 tablespoons Chef Kenny's Raging Cajun Spice, or other Cajun seasoning
1 teaspoon kosher salt

For the Gratin
Kosher Salt
1 pound medium pasta shells
4 cups Black Pepper Cheese Sauce, warmed (see left)
2 cups Pimento Cheese (see above)
4 ounces sharp Cheddar cheese, shredded (1 cup)
4 ounces Monterey Jack cheese, shredded (1 cup)
4 ounces pepper Jack cheese, shredded (1 cup)

FOR THE BUILD
Sliced scallions, for garnish
Chef Kenny's Raging Cajun Spice, or other Cajun seasoning for garnish

Make the BBQ Sauce

In a large bowl, whisk together the ketchup, apple cider vinegar, molasses, lemon juice, orange juice, brown sugar, Cajun spice blend, chicken seasoning, cinnamon, and salt. Cover and refrigerate until ready to use. (Leftover sauce can be stored in an airtight container in the refrigerator.)

Make the Chicken

1. Whisk the oil, chicken and Cajun seasonings, lemon juice, and salt in a large bowl.
2. Put the chicken legs in the bowl with the marinade and toss to thoroughly coat. Marinate the chicken, covered in the refrigerator, for a minimum of 2 hours and up to 12 hours.
3. Preheat a smoker or the oven to 350°F.
4. Place the chicken legs directly on the smoker or cook them on a sheet pan in the oven. Cook for 40 minutes, or until a meat thermometer inserted into the thickest part of the leg reaches 155°F.
5. Baste the chicken with the barbecue sauce. Cook the chicken 25 to 30 minutes longer, to an internal temperature of 165°F. If using a smoker, transfer the smoked chicken to a sheet pan. Cover the chicken with foil to keep warm.

Make the Mac & Cheese

Make the Black Pepper Cheese Sauce
1. Combine the half-and-half, lager, pepper, and salt in a medium saucepan and bring to a boil on medium-high heat.
2. Put the fried shallots, fried garlic, cream cheese, Colby Jack, Monterey Jack, pepper Jack, Cheddar, and xanthan gum in another medium saucepan.
3. Pour the half-and-half mixture over the cheese blend and allow the cheese to melt naturally for 3 to 5 minutes.
4. Over low heat, puree the cheese mixture with a handheld stick blender until smooth and warm throughout. Rewarm before assembling the mac & cheese.

Make the Pimento Cheese
1. Put the cottage cheese, cream cheese, Cheddar, Monterey Jack, sour cream, mustard barbecue sauce, Cajun spice blend, and salt in the bowl of a stand mixer with the paddle attachment (or you can combine the ingredients in a large bowl and mix with a spoon).
2. Mix on low speed for 30 seconds, then increase the speed to medium and mix for 1 minute, until thoroughly combined. Transfer to a bowl, cover, and refrigerate until ready to use.

Make the Gratin
1. Bring a large pot of salted water to a boil. Add the pasta and cook for 8 to 11 minutes, until just under al dente, stirring occasionally.
2. Drain the pasta and return it to the pot along with the rewarmed cheese sauce and the pimento cheese.

3. Cook on low to medium heat, stirring until the pimento cheese melts. Transfer the cheesy pasta to a large casserole. Preheat the broiler.
4. Toss together the cheddar, Monterey Jack, and pepper Jack in a medium bowl. Sprinkle the cheese blend over the pasta.
5. Place the casserole under the broiler for 1 to 2 minutes, or until the cheese is bubbling and golden brown.

The Build

1. Place a large scoop of mac & cheese in the center of a dinner plate. Sprinkle scallions over the mac & cheese. Place 2 chicken legs to one side of the mac & cheese.
2. Sprinkle a dash of Cajun spice over the chicken. Plate the remaining servings.

Lemon and Rosemary Roasted Chicken Breasts with Taleggio-Pancetta Mac & Cheese

Italian food is always a favorite—for American kids and adults alike. This dish is like fettuccine Alfredo, but with more flavor from the Taleggio and using rigatoni. Pasta is inexpensive and filling, and while we all probably have macaroni or shells or spaghetti in a box at home, this dish, like others in this chapter, is an opportunity to try new pasta shapes. Swap out your macaroni for orecchiette the next time you cook mac & cheese for a gathering, and it will impress.

INGREDIENTS

FOR THE LEMON-ROSEMARY CHICKEN

1 cup fresh lemon juice (about 6 lemons)

½ cup mild olive oil

¼ cup honey

4 to 6 sprigs rosemary, leaves only, chopped (½ cup)

12 cloves garlic, peeled

1 tablespoon kosher salt

1 teaspoon crushed red pepper

6 bone-in, skin-on chicken breasts

FOR THE MAC & CHEESE

For the Taleggio-Pancetta Cheese Sauce
Makes 8 cups

3 cups half-and-half

1 cup white wine, preferably pinot grigio or chardonnay

½ medium yellow or white onion, cut into small dice (½ cup)

½ cup small-diced fennel

10 cloves garlic

1 tablespoon kosher salt

1 pound Taleggio cheese, coarsely diced (2 cups)

1 cup mascarpone cheese

¼ teaspoon xanthan gum

1 pound pancetta or smoked bacon, finely chopped

For the Rosemary Breadcrumbs

2 cups coarsely cubed ciabatta bread

2 tablespoons minced garlic

2 or 3 sprigs rosemary, leaves only, chopped (¼ cup)

½ cup rendered pancetta fat, reserved from the Taleggio-Pancetta Cheese Sauce, warmed

1 teaspoon kosher salt

1 teaspoon freshly ground black pepper

For the Gratin

Kosher salt

1 pound rigatoni pasta

4 cups Taleggio-Pancetta Cheese Sauce (see left)

4 ounces mozzarella cheese, shredded (1 cup)

3½ ounces Asiago cheese, shredded (1 cup)

4 ounces provolone cheese, shredded (1 cup)

FOR THE GARNISH

Olive oil

3 lemons, halved

Fresh rosemary leaves

Make the Lemon-Rosemary Chicken

1. Put the lemon juice, olive oil, honey, rosemary, garlic, salt, and crushed red pepper in a blender and blend until smooth. Transfer 1½ cups of this marinade to a large bowl.
2. Put the chicken in the bowl with the marinade and toss to thoroughly coat. Marinate, covered in the refrigerator, for a minimum of 2 hours and up to 12 hours. Transfer the remaining marinade to an airtight container and refrigerate.
3. Preheat the oven to 350°F and line a sheet pan with foil.
4. Transfer the chicken from the marinade to the prepared sheet pan. Discard the marinade.
5. Roast the chicken on the middle rack for 30 minutes, or until a meat thermometer inserted in the thickest part of a breast reaches 145°F.
6. Baste the chicken with the reserved marinade and the pan drippings. Roast the chicken for another 10 to 12 minutes, or until it reaches an internal temperature of 165°F. Remove the chicken from the oven and cover with foil to keep warm.

Make the Taleggio-Pancetta Cheese Sauce

1. Combine the half-and-half, wine, onion, fennel, garlic, and salt in a medium saucepan and bring to a boil over high heat. Reduce the heat to medium-low and simmer for 10 to 15 minutes, or until the vegetables have softened.
2. Put the Taleggio, mascarpone, and xanthan gum in another medium saucepan.
3. Pour the half-and-half mixture over the cheese blend and allow it to melt naturally for 3 to 5 minutes.
4. Over low heat, puree the cheese mixture with a handheld stick blender until smooth.
5. Cook the pancetta in a skillet over medium heat until crispy and the fat has rendered. Use a slotted spoon to transfer the crispy pancetta to the cheese sauce and fold it in. Reserve the rendered pancetta fat (you should have about ½ cup).

Make the Rosemary Breadcrumbs

1. Preheat the oven to 350°F and line a sheet pan with foil.
2. In a medium bowl, toss together the ciabatta, garlic, rosemary, reserved rendered pancetta fat, salt, and pepper, then spread the bread cubes on the prepared sheet pan.
3. Bake for 20 minutes, stirring every 5 minutes or so. Cool, then place the toasted bread cubes in a food processor and pulse to a breadcrumb consistency. Set aside until ready to use.

Make the Gratin

1. Bring a large pot of salted water to a boil. Add the pasta and cook for 8 to 11 minutes, until just under al dente, stirring occasionally.
2. Drain the pasta and return it to the pot along with the rewarmed cheese sauce.
3. Cook on low to medium heat, stirring until the pasta and sauce are well mixed. Transfer the cheesy pasta to a large casserole. Preheat the broiler.
4. Toss together the mozzarella, Asiago, and provolone in a medium bowl. Sprinkle the cheese blend over the pasta.
5. Place the casserole under the broiler for 1 to 2 minutes, until the cheese is bubbling and golden brown.

Make the Garnish	1. Heat a medium cast-iron skillet or sauté pan on medium-high.
	2. Coat the pan lightly with olive oil. When the oil is hot, set the lemon halves in the skillet, cut side down. Cook for 1 to 2 minutes, until caramelized. Set aside until ready to plate.
The Build	1. Place a large scoop of mac & cheese in the center of a dinner plate. Sprinkle the breadcrumbs over the mac & cheese.
	2. Put a piece of chicken on one side of the mac & cheese and place a charred lemon half next to the chicken. Garnish with fresh rosemary leaves. Plate the remaining servings.

Chicken Wing Mole with Charred Corn– Jalapeño Mac & Cheese

I created a signature version of mole that is authentic to the culture, yet has a unique twist. Black beans are usually not an ingredient in moles, but I like the texture and the flavor of the beans in mine. Mole is a Mexican comfort food, and mac & cheese is an American comfort food. I created a dish here that speaks to the flavors of Mexico and celebrates their place on American tables.

INGREDIENTS

FOR THE BLACK BEAN MOLE

1 cup corn oil
1 medium yellow or white onion, sliced (1 cup)
10 cloves garlic, peeled
4 ounces butternut squash, peeled, seeded, and cut into large dice (1 cup)
1 ancho chile, stemmed
1 jalapeño pepper, stemmed and sliced
¼ cup canned chipotle in adobo sauce
½ medium red bell pepper, seeded and cut into small dice (½ cup)
2 bay leaves
¼ cup roasted pepitas
2 tablespoons Chef Kenny's Cinnamon Coffee Rub (to make your own, see page 16)
2 tablespoons Chef Kenny's Fried Chicken Seasoning, or other poultry seasoning
1 (15-ounce) can black beans with their liquid
¼ cup dried cranberries
2 cups low-sodium chicken stock
½ cup bittersweet dark chocolate chips or grated bar
Kosher salt

FOR THE CHICKEN

½ cup corn oil
2 tablespoons Chef Kenny's Fried Chicken Seasoning, or other poultry seasoning
Kosher salt
24 jumbo chicken wings
4 cups Black Bean Mole (see above)
1 cup low-sodium chicken stock

FOR THE MAC & CHEESE

For the Charred Corn
Makes 4 cups

6 ears corn, shucked
½ cup corn oil
3 tablespoons kosher salt

Charred Jalapeño Queso
Makes 6 cups

4 jalapeño peppers, stemmed
4 ounces (½ block) cream cheese
4 ounces pepper Jack cheese, shredded (1 cup)
4 ounces Monterey Jack cheese, shredded (1 cup)
¼ teaspoon xanthan gum
3 cups half-and-half
1 cup Modelo beer, or any amber or lager
½ yellow onion, cut into small dice (½ cup)
½ cup small-diced fennel
10 cloves garlic
1 tablespoon kosher salt

For the Gratin
Kosher salt
1 pound farfalle pasta
4 cups Charred Jalapeño Queso (see above)
3 cups Charred Corn (see above)
6 ounces Monterey Jack cheese, shredded (1½ cups)
6 ounces pepper Jack cheese, shredded (1½ cups)

FOR THE BUILD
Crumbled Cotija cheese, for garnish
Fresh cilantro leaves, for garnish
Sliced jalapeño pepper, for garnish

Make the Black Bean Mole

1. Heat a large saucepan on medium-high. Once warm, add the corn oil and heat for 1 minute.
2. Cook the onion, garlic, butternut squash, ancho chile, jalapeño, chipotle, bell pepper, bay leaves, and pepitas in the saucepan, stirring, for 1 minute.
3. Add the cinnamon coffee rub and chicken seasoning and cook for 1 minute, then add the black beans and cranberries and cook for 5 minutes, stirring regularly.
4. Pour in the stock and reduce the heat to medium-low. Cook for 20 minutes, until the vegetables are tender.
5. Stir the chocolate into the sauce to melt, then stir in salt to taste. Remove the bay leaves and discard. Puree with a handheld stick blender until smooth. Set aside.

Make the Chicken

1. Whisk the oil, chicken seasoning, and salt to taste in a large bowl.
2. Put the chicken wings in the marinade and toss to coat. Marinate the chicken, covered in the refrigerator, for a minimum of 2 hours and up to 12 hours.
3. Preheat the oven to 425°F.
4. Remove the chicken wings from the marinade and place in a large casserole. Roast the wings for 15 minutes.
5. While the wings roast, put 4 cups of the mole and stock in a medium saucepan and bring to a simmer over medium-low heat.
6. Pour the mole-stock sauce over the wings and toss to evenly coat the chicken and submerge it in the sauce.
7. Cover the casserole with a layer of parchment paper, then top with foil.
8. Bake for an additional 15 minutes, then let rest for 20 minutes before serving. Switch the oven to broil.

Make the Mac & Cheese

Make the Charred Corn

1. Line a sheet pan with foil.
2. Toss the corn with the oil and salt in a large bowl.
3. Transfer the corn to the prepared sheet pan and broil, rotating regularly, until evenly charred, about 10 minutes. Keep the broiler on to char the jalapeños.
4. When the corn is cool enough to handle, cut the kernels off the cobs and set aside.

Make the Charred Jalapeño Queso

1. Line a sheet pan with foil.
2. Put the jalapeño on the prepared sheet pan and broil until the peppers are charred on all sides, about 8 minutes. Put the charred jalapeños, cream cheese, pepper Jack cheese, Monterey Jack cheese, and xanthan gum in a medium saucepan.
3. Bring the half-and-half, beer, onion, fennel, garlic, and salt to a boil on medium-high heat. Reduce the heat to medium-low and simmer for 10 to 15 minutes, or until the vegetables are soft.
4. Add the half-and-half mixture to the jalapeño and cheeses and allow the cheeses to melt naturally for 3 to 5 minutes.

5. Over low heat, puree the cheese mixture with a handheld stick blender until smooth. Rewarm before assembling the mac & cheese. (Leftover queso can be stored in an airtight container in the refrigerator.)

Make the Gratin

1. Bring a large pot of salted water to a boil. Add the pasta and cook for 8 to 11 minutes, until just under al dente, stirring occasionally.
2. Drain the pasta and return it to the pot along with the rewarmed queso. Cook on medium-low heat, stirring to thoroughly mix the sauce and pasta.
3. Transfer the cheesy pasta to a large casserole and fold in the charred corn. Preheat the broiler.
4. Toss together the Monterey Jack and pepper Jack in a medium bowl. Sprinkle the cheese blend over the pasta.
5. Place the casserole under the broiler for 1 to 2 minutes, until the cheese is bubbling and golden brown.

The Build

1. Place a large scoop of mac & cheese in the center of a dinner plate. Put several chicken wings to the side of the mac & cheese.
2. Sprinkle the Cotija cheese over the chicken wings and then sprinkle with fresh cilantro leaves and sliced jalapeños. Plate the remaining servings.

Bulgogi-Style Grilled Chicken Thighs with Asparagus-Spinach Mac & Cheese

I love Korean food. In the 1990s, a cook from Korea took me to eat at a Korean restaurant in Jacksonville, Florida. He talked through what to order and how to eat it—and it is still what I order to this day: marinated short rib with pork belly and shrimp, and then all the fixings, including kimchi, marinated tofu, sticky sesame sweet potato, baby eels or sardines, and gochujang with sesame oil, lemon, and black pepper. It was my first experience with Korean food, and now Korean restaurants are some of my favorites to explore. I love bulgogi and the whole family-style aspect of grilling your own food—and the meats are always super flavorful.

SERVES 6

FOR THE BULGOGI-MARINATED CHICKEN
2 Asian pears, quartered and cored
1 bunch scallions, coarsely chopped
10 cloves garlic
1 cup rice vinegar
½ cup gochujang (Korean fermented chile and bean paste)
¼ cup sesame oil
2 tablespoons kosher salt
12 boneless, skinless chicken thighs

FOR THE ASPARAGUS AND ASIAN PEAR
Sesame or olive oil, if needed
1 bunch jumbo asparagus, tough ends removed
2 Asian pears, quartered and cored

FOR THE MAC & CHEESE

For the Fried Garlic–Cheese Sauce
3 cups half-and-half
1 cup lager
1 tablespoon kosher salt
1 cup fried garlic, preferably Maesri
2 tablespoons ground ginger
2 ounces Monterey Jack cheese, shredded (½ cup)
2 (8-ounce) blocks cream cheese
¼ teaspoon xanthan gum

For the Gratin
Kosher salt
1 pound penne pasta
2 cups loosely packed baby spinach
6 ounces Monterey Jack cheese, shredded (1½ cups)
6 ounces mozzarella cheese, shredded (1½ cups)

FOR THE BUILD
Slivered scallions, for garnish
Gochujang honey (recipe page 36), for garnish
Sesame or benne seeds, for garnish

Make the Bulgogi-Marinated Chicken

1. Put the Asian pears, scallions, garlic, rice vinegar, gochujang, sesame oil, and salt in a blender and blend until smooth. Transfer the marinade to a large bowl.
2. Put the chicken in the bowl with half of the marinade, toss to coat evenly, and marinate, covered in the refrigerator, for a minimum of 2 hours and up to 12 hours. Transfer the remaining marinade to an airtight container and refrigerate until ready to use.
3. Preheat a gas or charcoal grill to medium-high heat or heat a cast-iron skillet over medium-high heat on the stove. Remove the chicken from the marinade and place on the grill or in the skillet; reserve the marinade.
4. Cook the chicken on one side for 6 minutes, then turn and cook on the other side for another 6 minutes, or until a meat thermometer inserted in the thickest part of a thigh reads 165°F. While grilling, baste the chicken with the reserved marinade to keep moist.
5. Transfer the chicken to a plate and cover with foil to keep warm until ready to serve.

Make the Asparagus and Asian Pear

1. Preheat a gas or charcoal grill to medium-high heat, or a cast-iron skillet coated lightly with sesame or olive oil on medium-high heat on the stove.
2. Place the asparagus and Asian pears on the grill and cook for 1 to 2 minutes on each side, until lightly charred. Alternatively, cook on the stove until browned and tender.
3. Allow the asparagus and Asian pears to cool to room temperature. Slice the asparagus into bite-sized pieces and set aside with the Asian pears. Cover with foil to keep warm.

Make the Mac & Cheese

Make the Fried Garlic-Cheese Sauce

1. Combine the half-and-half, beer, and salt in a medium saucepan over high heat and bring to a boil.
2. Put the fried garlic, ginger, Monterey Jack, cream cheese, and xanthan gum in another medium saucepan.
3. Pour the half-and-half mixture over the cheese blend and allow it to melt naturally for 3 to 5 minutes.
4. Over low heat, puree the cheese sauce with a handheld stick blender until smooth.

Make the Gratin

1. Bring a large pot of salted water to a boil. Add the pasta and cook for 8 to 11 minutes, until just under al dente, stirring occasionally.
2. Drain the pasta and return it to the pot along with the rewarmed cheese sauce and the spinach.
3. Cook on low heat, stirring to fully incorporate the pasta, cheese sauce, and spinach. Transfer the cheesy pasta to a large casserole. Preheat the broiler.
4. Toss together the Monterey Jack and mozzarella in a medium bowl. Sprinkle the cheese blend over the pasta.
5. Place the casserole under the broiler for 1 to 2 minutes, until the cheese is bubbling and golden brown.

The Build

1. Put a large scoop of mac & cheese in the center of a dinner plate. Slice the chicken thighs into strips. Place several strips to one side of the mac & cheese.
2. Place grilled asparagus and Asian pear on the plate and garnish with scallions.
3. Drizzle gochujang honey over the chicken and sprinkle with sesame seeds. Plate the remaining servings.

Port-Glazed Chicken Thighs with Saint André–White Truffle Mac & Cheese

This is the Rolls-Royce of mac & cheeses. It is a French preparation, decadent and delicious. If you want to flex with a mac & cheese, this is the one to make. The chicken is prepared in a coq au vin style and paired with the Saint André–truffle mac & cheese—in other words a very decadent dish. Truffle is a common ingredient in European fine dining, and it brings an umami flavor that is very distinctive and both rich and elegant. It actually adds a little smokiness to the cheese sauce. White truffle is more perfumy and delicate, and here it doesn't overpower the cheese. This meal calls for a big red wine, because in European households, there is always wine on the table at dinner.

INGREDIENTS

SERVES 6

FOR THE CHICKEN

6 bone-in, skin-on chicken thighs

1 tablespoon kosher salt, plus more if needed

1 teaspoon freshly ground black pepper, plus more if needed

½ cup olive oil

4 tablespoons (½ stick) salted butter

5 ounces carrots, cut into medium dice (1 cup)

1 cup medium-diced fennel

1 medium yellow or white onion, cut into medium dice (1 cup)

¼ cup chopped garlic, plus 20 whole peeled cloves

1 bunch thyme

1 (750-ml) bottle ruby port

4 cups low-sodium chicken stock

¼ teaspoon xanthan gum

FOR THE MAC & CHEESE

For the Saint André–White Truffle Sauce

3 cups half-and-half

1 cup white wine, preferably chardonnay

4 ounces shallots, cut into small dice (½ cup)

¼ cup small-diced fennel

2 tablespoons chopped garlic

1 tablespoon kosher salt

1 pound Saint André cheese, cubed (2 cups)

1 cup mascarpone cheese

2 tablespoons white truffle oil

¼ teaspoon xanthan gum

For the Gratin

Kosher salt

1 pound cavatappi pasta

6 ounces Monterey Jack cheese, shredded (1½ cups)

4 ounces truffle Gouda cheese, shredded (1½ cups), or 4 ounces Gouda cheese, shredded (1½ cups), plus 2 tablespoons white truffle oil

FOR THE BUILD

Fresh thyme leaves, for garnish

1 bunch scallions, sliced, for garnish

Make the Chicken

1. Season the chicken thighs with the salt and pepper.
2. Heat a rondeau or large skillet over medium-high. Heat the olive oil in the pan for 1 minute.
3. Transfer the chicken to the pan, skin side down, and cook for 3 minutes. Flip the chicken and cook for another 3 minutes. Remove to a plate and set aside.
4. Melt the butter in the same skillet and add the carrots, fennel, onion, and garlic and cook for 10 minutes, until the vegetables start to caramelize.
5. Return the chicken to the pan and add the thyme. Deglaze the skillet with the port and scrape up all the good bits from the bottom of the pan.
6. Pour in the stock and cover with a lid. Reduce the heat to medium-low and simmer the chicken for 30 minutes, or until a meat thermometer registers 165°F.
7. Stir in the xanthan gum to thicken the sauce, and season with additional salt and pepper, if needed.

Make the Mac & Cheese

Make the Saint André–White Truffle Sauce

1. Combine the half-and-half, white wine, shallot, fennel, garlic, and salt in a medium saucepan and bring to a boil over high heat.
2. Put the Saint André, mascarpone, white truffle oil, and xanthan gum in another medium saucepan.
3. Pour the half-and-half mixture over the cheese blend and allow the cheese to melt naturally for 3 to 5 minutes.
4. Over low heat, puree the cheese mixture with a handheld stick blender until smooth. Cover to keep warm while the pasta cooks.

Make the Gratin

1. Bring a large pot of salted water to a boil. Add the pasta and cook for 8 to 11 minutes, until just under al dente, stirring occasionally.
2. Drain the pasta and return it to the pot along with the warm Saint André–white truffle sauce.
3. Cook on low to medium heat, stirring to thoroughly combine the pasta and sauce. Transfer the cheesy pasta to a large casserole. Preheat the broiler.
4. Toss together the Monterey Jack and truffle Gouda in a medium bowl. Sprinkle the cheese blend over the pasta.
5. Place the casserole under the broiler for 1 to 2 minutes, until the cheese is bubbling and golden brown.

The Build

Place a large scoop of mac & cheese in the center of a dinner plate. Put a chicken thigh on one side of the mac & cheese. Spoon port sauce over the chicken thigh. Garnish with fresh thyme leaves and scallions. Plate the remaining servings.

FISH + GRITS

SOUTHERN FRIED CATFISH WITH SWEET CORN GRITS

A classic Southern preparation of catfish dipped in a
seasoned cornmeal dredge, fried, and served with creamy grits
with corn and homemade hot sauce

176

PLANCHA-STYLE BRANZINO WITH MASCARPONE POLENTA

A Spanish preparation of branzino over decadent polenta
with melted tomatoes, fennel, and basil

180

FRANCHAISE OF GROUPER WITH TRUFFLE CHEESE GRITS

An Italian preparation with a side of truffle Gouda
cheese grits and garlic spinach

184

MISO HONEY–GLAZED SCOTTISH SALMON
WITH BAMBOO RICE GRITS

Asian-inspired salmon served with bamboo rice grits,
charred baby bok choy, fermented black beans, and sesame seeds

188

BAJAN-STYLE CREOLE FISH WITH OKRA POLENTA

An inspired take on the national dish of Barbados, with cou cou
(okra polenta), tomato pepper sauce, and Bajan hot sauce

192

My grandmother taught me how to fish. My mother's family was from St. Augustine, Florida, and on our visits, we would go fishing as a family: my brother, me, my uncle, my cousins, and Grandma. We would grab poles, pick up some shrimp as bait, find some water like a neighborhood pond, and fish for a few hours.

Growing up in Cleveland, I didn't fish all that much at home, but we ate fried fish and grits all the time. I ate grits every day for breakfast. During the winter, my mom would fry up some perch in the morning. She would make a little bowl out of foil, fill it with fish and grits and some hot sauce on top, and it was a hot breakfast that kept us warm as we walked to the bus stop in the cold.

Fish, grits, and fried green tomatoes were regulars on our dinner menu at home during the summer months. Mom always had tomato vines growing in the backyard, and she liked to pick them when they were green. She would slice and fry them dredged in cornmeal along with the fish. She would cook a big pile of perch or walleye pike, because that was what was caught fresh where we lived.

Catfish is my favorite. I love it. Since it is a bottom-feeder, it has a sort of earthiness to its flavor. It is a fish that holds spice very well and is versatile to cook with. Sturgeon is also a favorite. It is like a large catfish, but with more oil in its meat. I think of it as the Rolls-Royce of the bottom-feeder fish. It has a lot of flavor and is delicious. Snapper, black bass, branzino, and turbot are all at the top of my list as well.

When buying fish, do some research on what is caught where you live, and what season it runs. This will be the freshest fish at any local fish market. If there are no nearby fish markets, the next best choice is a sustainably sourced fish from your local grocery store. Online, there are many resources to guide you on selecting fish caught using sustainable methods. When you buy fish whole, you can easily tell if it's fresh: Its eyes will be clear, it will be firm, and it will have little to no smell. It's worth learning how to break down a fish, but you can also ask the fishmonger to fillet it for you. Use the internet to find out what's in season and go from there.

When I was cooking in Barbados, I learned how to make their national dish, flying fish over cou cou, which is best described as an okra-based polenta. Flying fish isn't something easily found in American fish markets, but the preparation of the fish in the Caribbean is very similar to the franchaise of grouper, an Italian preparation that I learned from a mentor, Chef Matthew Medure, and in this chapter it is presented with truffle Gouda cheese grits. No matter the coastal culture, one thing rings true—a crispy fried protein, in this case fish, goes well with any creamy grain. The lightness of the fish and the creaminess of the porridge make for a well-balanced dish.

Southern Fried Catfish with Sweet Corn Grits

From Barbados to Cleveland, Ohio, in Black culture, fried fish is often eaten with hot sauce. This dish celebrates the classic Southern preparation of fried fish, cheese grits, and hot sauce. I have been making grits since I was five years old. The key to making good grits is to soak them for several hours before cooking them and to start the cooking with seasoned water: Add salt and butter to the boiling water, then add the grits. The grits will bloom out in the water and absorb the salt.

INGREDIENTS

FOR THE HOT SAUCE

Makes 8 cups

10 habanero peppers

1 cup roasted red peppers (from a
    12-ounce can)

1 medium yellow or white onion, sliced (1 cup)

10 cloves garlic, peeled

½ cup kosher salt

2 cups water

4 cups apple cider vinegar

¼ teaspoon xanthan gum

FOR THE GRITS

¾ cup stone-ground grits, or quick grits

1 cup water, plus more for soaking the grits

1 cup heavy cream

4 tablespoons (½ stick) salted butter

1 cup corn kernels cut from cobs
    (from about 2 medium ears)

1 tablespoon kosher salt

¼ teaspoon ground white pepper

¼ cup (4 tablespoons) cream cheese

¼ cup shredded pepper Jack cheese

FOR THE CHARRED LEMON

Olive oil, for the pan

3 lemons, halved

FOR THE CATFISH

1 cup buttermilk

4 large eggs

¼ cup Chef Kenny's Raging Cajun Spice,
    or other Cajun seasoning

1 tablespoon plus ¼ cup Chef Kenny's Fried
    Chicken Seasoning, or other poultry seasoning

6 (4- to 6-ounce) catfish fillets

4 cups canola oil

2 cups fine cornmeal

1 cup self-rising flour

½ cup cornstarch

½ cup rice flour

FOR THE BUILD

Watercress, for garnish

Make the Hot Sauce

1. Place the habanero and roasted red peppers, onion, garlic, salt, and water in a blender and puree until smooth.
2. Transfer the puree to a plastic container and cover with plastic wrap. Use a toothpick to poke holes in the plastic wrap. Place on your countertop, away from direct sunlight, and ferment for at least 24 hours and up to 7 days.
3. Put the pepper mash into a medium saucepan and stir in the apple cider vinegar. Bring the mixture to a boil on medium-high heat, then reduce the heat to medium-low and simmer for 10 minutes.
4. Add the xanthan gum and puree with a handheld stick blender until the sauce is smooth.
5. Strain through a fine-mesh strainer into an airtight container and set aside in the refrigerator. The solids can be saved: they are a homemade sambal (chile paste) that you can use to spice up marmalades, dressings, and marinades. The sambal will keep in an airtight container in the refrigerator for up to 6 months. The hot sauce will keep for many months as well.

Make the Grits

1. Put the grits in a quart-sized container. Cover the grits with water and top with a lid. Place in the refrigerator to soak for at least 12 hours and up to 24 hours.
2. Place 1 cup water, the cream, butter, corn, and salt into a medium saucepan. Bring to a simmer on medium-high heat.
3. Drain the presoaked grits and add them to the simmering cream mixture while whisking constantly until mixed.
4. Reduce the heat to low and cook for 20 to 25 minutes, stirring occasionally, until the grits are creamy.
5. Add the white pepper, cream cheese, and pepper Jack cheese. Mix thoroughly until the cheese is melted.
6. Keep warm, covered, until ready to serve.

Make the Charred Lemon

1. Heat a medium cast-iron or other heavy-bottomed skillet on medium-high. Coat the pan lightly with olive oil.
2. Cook the lemon halves, cut side down in the pan, for 1 to 2 minutes, or until caramelized.
3. Reserve until ready to use.

Make the Catfish

1. Place the buttermilk, eggs, Cajun spice, and 1 tablespoon of the chicken seasoning in a large bowl and whisk thoroughly.
2. Add the catfish fillets and let marinate for 20 minutes at room temperature and up to 24 hours, covered, in the refrigerator.
3. When ready to fry the fish, heat the oil in a 14- or 16-inch cast-iron skillet on medium for 20 minutes, or until it comes to 325° to 350°F.
4. Put the cornmeal, self-rising flour, cornstarch, rice flour, and the ¼ cup fried chicken seasoning in a medium bowl and whisk to thoroughly combine.

5. Working with one fillet at a time, transfer the fish from the buttermilk marinade into the cornmeal dredge and thoroughly coat on both sides, pressing the dredge into the fish. Set on a large plate.

6. Once you have two or three fillets coated, carefully place them in the hot oil. Cook the fillets for 3 minutes, then flip them and cook for another 3 minutes on the other side. Avoid overcrowding the skillet.

7. Turn one more time and cook for an additional 1 to 2 minutes, or until golden brown and crispy. Transfer the cooked fillets to a sheet pan and keep warm in a low (170°F) oven.

The Build

Place a heaping scoop of grits in the center of a plate. Put a catfish fillet on top of the grits. Add a drizzle of hot sauce to taste. Garnish with a charred lemon half and watercress. Plate the remaining servings.

Plancha-Style Branzino with Mascarpone Polenta

Branzino is a European sea bass that is a regular on Italian menus and throughout the Mediterranean. This is a Spanish preparation in the plancha style, which means to cook on a hot, flat surface. This could be a griddle, a piece of cedar, or, in this case, a searingly hot skillet.

The polenta is a creamy-style porridge made with fine cornmeal or semolina. I finish mine with mascarpone cheese. The subtle flavor and creaminess of the mascarpone complement the fish beautifully. One of my favorite ways to cook vegetables is slowly, covered, on the stovetop. The aroma as they "melt" is intoxicating.

INGREDIENTS

SERVES 6

FOR THE MELTED TOMATOES
2 pints heirloom cherry tomatoes, or
    4 medium heirloom tomatoes, halved
1 bulb fennel, shaved (1 cup)
1 medium onion, shaved (1 cup)
½ cup halved, pitted kalamata olives
12 fresh basil leaves
10 cloves garlic, thinly sliced
1 tablespoon kosher salt
Pinch of crushed red pepper
½ cup extra-virgin olive oil
1 cup V8 juice

FOR THE POLENTA
2 cups water
1 cup heavy cream
4 tablespoons (½ stick) salted butter
1 tablespoon kosher salt
1 cup fine cornmeal or semolina
1 teaspoon freshly ground white pepper
½ cup mascarpone cheese

FOR THE BRANZINO
1 cup mild olive oil
6 (4- to 6-ounce) branzino fillets, skin on
2 tablespoons fennel pollen
2 tablespoons kosher salt

FOR THE BUILD
Thinly sliced fresh basil leaves

Make the Melted Tomatoes

1. Layer the tomatoes, fennel, onion, kalamata olives, basil, and garlic in a large skillet. Season with the salt and crushed red pepper, then add the olive oil and V8 juice.
2. Tent the skillet with parchment paper and cook on medium heat. Bring to a simmer, then reduce the heat to low.
3. Simmer for 20 minutes, or until the mixture melts together. Cover to keep warm.

Make the Polenta

1. Bring the water, cream, butter, and salt to a simmer in a medium saucepan over medium-high heat.
2. Add the cornmeal and whisk constantly until well mixed.
3. Reduce the heat to low and cook for 20 to 25 minutes, stirring constantly.
4. Once the polenta is fully cooked, add the white pepper and mascarpone cheese. Sir until the cheese is melted and the mixture is thoroughly incorporated. Cover to keep warm.

Make the Branzino

1. Heat the olive oil in a 14- or 16-inch nonstick skillet on medium-low for 3 minutes.
2. Place the branzino in the skillet, skin side down. (You will need to work in batches.) Place another clean skillet or pot, weighed down with cans, on top of the fillets to keep the fillets flat.
3. Increase the heat to medium and cook for about 5 minutes. Carefully remove the cans and top pan (they will be hot) and check to be sure the skin is crispy and the fish is cooked just past translucent. If it isn't, cook for a few minutes more.
4. Season the tops of the fish with fennel pollen and salt. Flip the fish and season the skin sides with fennel pollen and salt. Transfer the cooked fillets to a sheet pan and place in a low (170°F) oven to keep warm. Cook the remaining fillets in the same way.

The Build

Place a heaping scoop of polenta in the center of a plate. Top the polenta with some of the melted tomatoes and their broth. Put 1 branzino fillet on top of the tomatoes and sprinkle with sliced basil leaves. Plate the remaining servings.

Franchaise of Grouper with Truffle Cheese Grits

Grouper is a heavier, meatier fish that stands up well to stronger flavors, such as the Gouda and truffle in the grits here. Franchaise is an Italian cooking preparation where you dredge fish, chicken, or veal in a seasoned flour, then coat it with a little Parmesan-egg batter. You finish by searing it in butter or olive oil and braising the fish as it cooks with stock and a little cream or other dairy. Grouper is a great fish for this method of cooking, and it pairs well with the cheese grits. The fillets will need to be trench-cut, which your fishmonger can do for you.

SERVES 6

FOR THE TRUFFLE CHEESE GRITS

1 cup water

1 cup heavy cream

4 tablespoons (½ stick) salted butter

1 tablespoon black truffle oil

1 tablespoon kosher salt

¾ cup stone-ground grits, soaked overnight in 1 cup water (see page 178)

8 ounces truffle Gouda cheese, cubed (3 cups), or 8 ounces smoked Gouda, cubed (3 cups), with 2 tablespoons white truffle oil

1 teaspoon freshly ground white pepper

FOR THE GARLIC SPINACH

½ cup mild olive oil

10 cloves garlic, sliced

4 ounces shallots or small white onions, sliced (½ cup)

Pinch of crushed red pepper

6 cups baby spinach

1 tablespoon kosher salt

Juice of 1 lemon (2 tablespoons)

FOR THE FRANCHAISE OF GROUPER

3 cups heavy cream

6 large eggs

8 ounces Parmesan cheese, grated (½ cup)

¼ bunch flat-leaf parsley, leaves chopped (¼ cup)

1 tablespoon kosher salt

1 cup self-rising flour

½ cup cornstarch

½ cup rice flour

¼ cup Chef Kenny's Fried Chicken Seasoning, or other poultry seasoning

1 cup mild olive oil

6 (4- to 6-ounce) grouper fillets, trench-cut (see above)

1 pound prosciutto di Parma, ground or finely chopped (1 cup)

5 cloves garlic, sliced

2 shallots or small white onions, sliced (½ cup)

1 cup low-sodium chicken stock

Make the Truffle Cheese Grits

1. Simmer the water, cream, butter, truffle oil, and salt in a medium saucepan over medium-high heat.
2. Drain the presoaked grits and add them to the simmering cream mixture while whisking constantly until mixed.
3. Reduce the heat to low and cook for 20 to 25 minutes, stirring occasionally, until the grits are creamy.
4. Add the truffle Gouda and white pepper. Mix thoroughly until the cheese is melted. Cover to keep warm.

Make the Garlic Spinach

1. Heat a large skillet on medium. Add the olive oil, garlic, and shallots. Sauté, stirring frequently, until the garlic and shallots have softened, about 1 minute. Add the crushed red pepper and toast lightly.
2. Add the spinach and sauté until wilted, about 2 minutes. Season with salt and finish with the fresh lemon juice. Cover to keep warm.

Make the Franchaise of Grouper

1. Whisk 1 cup of the cream, the eggs, Parmesan, parsley, and salt in a medium bowl.
2. Combine the self-rising flour, cornstarch, rice flour, and chicken seasoning in another medium bowl.
3. Heat the olive oil in a 14- or 16-inch nonstick skillet over medium-low for 3 minutes.
4. Work with one piece of fish at a time and place it in the flour mixture and then into the cream and egg mixture, coating the fish on both sides. Set aside on a plate. Repeat for the remaining fillets.
5. Put two or three pieces of fish in the pan and cook on one side for 3 minutes. Flip the fish and cook on the other side for 3 minutes. Transfer the fish to a large plate. (The fillets will not be fully cooked, and that's okay. They will cook another few minutes in the sauce.) Repeat with the remaining fillets.
6. Clean out any bits from the pan and add the prosciutto, garlic, and shallots. Cook for 1 minute, then add the remaining 2 cups cream and the stock. Scrape all the brown bits from the bottom of the pan into the stock and cream. Stir for about 30 seconds, until the sauce is combined.
7. Increase the heat to high and bring the sauce to a boil, then reduce the heat to medium-low and bring to a simmer. Place the grouper back in the pan and coat with the sauce. Cook for 5 to 7 minutes, or until the sauce reduces by half and the fish is tender.

The Build

Place a heaping scoop of grits in the center of a plate and top with a piece of grouper and some sauce. Put the garlic spinach to one side of the grouper and grits. Plate the remaining servings.

Miso Honey–Glazed Scottish Salmon with Bamboo Rice Grits

The miso-honey marinade here is a Japanese-style cure that is usually used with cod. I chose salmon for this preparation, but any type of fatty fish—cod, trout, mahi-mahi—will work. The marinade caramelizes as the fish broils and its richness complements the fattiness of the fish and the bamboo rice. Bamboo rice has a light green color because it's infused with chlorophyll from bamboo. Similar to grits, it should be soaked overnight before cooking. It is a short-grain rice that becomes creamy when it cooks, much like a risotto. It is wonderfully unique and worth seeking out to try. The flavor of the rice is herbaceous and slightly nutty and is a great pairing with the salmon. This dish highlights a lot of classic Asian flavors, such as miso, and is an opportunity to get out of your comfort zone and try something new.

SERVES 6

FOR THE SALMON
1 cup honey
1 cup white miso paste
¼ cup sake
¼ cup low-sodium soy sauce
2 egg yolks
6 (5-ounce) skinless Scottish salmon fillets, or other fresh salmon
¼ cup sesame oil

FOR THE BAMBOO RICE
2 cups water
1 cup canned coconut milk, preferably Thai Kitchen
4 tablespoons (½ stick) salted butter
2 tablespoons ground ginger
1 tablespoon kosher salt
¾ cup bamboo rice, soaked overnight (see page 178 for how to soak grits)
1 teaspoon freshly ground white pepper

FOR THE BOK CHOY
¼ cup sesame oil
6 baby bok choy, halved
1 cup water
½ cup rice vinegar
1 tablespoon kosher salt

FOR THE BUILD
½ cup gochujang honey (recipe on page 36)
¼ cup Chinese douchi (fermented black beans)
2 tablespoons benne or sesame seeds

**Make the
Salmon Marinade**

1. Whisk the honey, miso, sake, soy sauce, and egg yolks in a large bowl. Add the salmon fillets and coat in the marinade.
2. Place the salmon and marinade in an airtight container and marinate for 6 to 12 hours in the refrigerator.

**Make the
Bamboo Rice**

1. Simmer the water, coconut milk, butter, ginger, and salt in a medium saucepan over medium-high heat.
2. Drain the presoaked rice and add it to the simmering cream mixture, stirring constantly until well mixed.
3. Reduce the heat to low and cook, uncovered, for 20 to 25 minutes, stirring occasionally, until the rice is creamy. Once the rice is fully cooked, add the white pepper. Cover to keep warm.

Make the Bok Choy

1. Heat a large skillet on medium heat, then pour in the sesame oil.
2. Sear the baby bok choy in the skillet, cut side down, for 3 minutes. Flip the bok choy and cook for another 3 minutes.
3. Whisk the water and rice vinegar in a small bowl. Add this mixture to the skillet and deglaze the pan, scraping any brown bits from the bottom. Cook for 30 seconds.
4. Turn off the heat and cover with a lid. Let the bok choy steam for 1 minute.
5. Transfer the bok choy and any liquid to a plate. Season with salt and cover with foil to keep warm.

Make the Salmon

1. Preheat the broiler. Line a sheet pan with foil and coat with half of the sesame oil.
2. Put the salmon on the oiled pan, top side down.
3. Place the pan on the middle rack of the oven and broil for 8 minutes, or until the tops are browned and caramelized. Drizzle with the remaining sesame oil.

The Build

1. Place a heaping scoop of bamboo rice in the center of a plate and top with some of the baby bok choy. Place a piece of salmon on top of the bok choy.
2. Drizzle the gochujang honey over the fish, bok choy, and rice. Sprinkle with douchi. Finish with a pinch of benne seeds. Plate the remaining servings.

Bajan-Style Creole Fish with Okra Polenta

This is my take on the national dish of Barbados, and a tribute to the country's history and culture. It is traditionally served with flying fish, but mahi-mahi is also a fish that runs in their waters and is much easier to find in fish markets in other parts of the world. The fish is served over cou cou, a dish made from cornmeal and okra. As the okra cooks, it releases its starchy slime, but the slime, usually not the most appealing characteristic of the vegetable, actually creates the creaminess in the cornmeal and has a mouthfeel similar to grits with cheese and butter. Okra is native to West Africa, and it is thought that enslaved people originally brought it to America and the Caribbean. Now it is a staple of Southern cuisine.

SERVES 6

INGREDIENTS

FOR THE BAJAN HOT SAUCE

1 cup homemade hot sauce (recipe on
    page 176)
1 cup yellow mustard
¼ cup ground ginger
8 cloves garlic, peeled
¼ teaspoon xanthan gum

FOR THE COU COU

4 cups water
4 cloves garlic, chopped (1 tablespoon)
1 tablespoon kosher salt
1 teaspoon freshly ground white pepper
12 okra pods, sliced crosswise (1 cup)
¾ cup fine cornmeal

FOR THE MAHI-MAHI

1 cup heavy cream
6 large eggs
¼ bunch marjoram, chopped (¼ cup)
1 tablespoon kosher salt
1 cup self-rising flour
½ cup cornstarch
½ cup rice flour
¼ cup Chef Kenny's Fried Chicken Seasoning,
    or other poultry seasoning
1¼ cups mild olive oil
6 (4- to 6-ounce) mahi-mahi fillets
1 zucchini, coarsely diced (1 cup)
1 medium red bell pepper, seeded and
    coarsely diced (1 cup)
5 cloves garlic, sliced
2 shallots, sliced
1 cup tomato juice
1 cup spicy V8 Juice

FOR THE BUILD

1 bunch watercress

Make the Bajan Hot Sauce

1. Combine the hot sauce, mustard, ginger, garlic, and xanthan gum in a small saucepan. Bring to a simmer over medium heat. Reduce the heat to low and simmer for 15 minutes.
2. Puree with a handheld stick blender, then strain the sauce through a fine-mesh sieve into a mason jar with tight-fitting lid. Refrigerate until ready to use. (The sauce can be made ahead and kept in the refrigerator for several months.)

Make the Cou Cou

1. Put the water, garlic, salt, and white pepper in a medium saucepan and bring to a boil on high heat.
2. Add the okra and cook for 1 minute. Use a slotted spoon to transfer the okra to a bowl.
3. Pour the cornmeal into the saucepan and whisk constantly. Reduce the heat to low and continue whisking for 5 minutes.
4. Return the okra to the saucepan and continue to stir the okra and cornmeal until thoroughly combined. Cover to keep warm.

Make the Mahi-Mahi

1. Whisk the cream, eggs, marjoram, and salt in a medium bowl.
2. Combine the self-rising flour, cornstarch, rice flour, and chicken seasoning in another medium bowl.
3. Heat 1 cup of the olive oil in a 14- or 16-inch nonstick skillet over medium for 3 minutes.
4. While the oil heats, place a mahi-mahi fillet in the flour mixture, dredging both sides, then place in the cream mixture to coat. Set aside on a plate. Continue with the remaining fillets.
5. Place two or three fillets in the hot oil and cook on one side for 3 minutes. Flip the fish and cook on the other side for 3 minutes. Transfer the fillets to a large plate and cook the remaining pieces. (The fish will not be fully cooked at this point, and that's okay. It will finish cooking in the sauce.)
6. Clean out any bits from the pan and add the remaining ¼ cup olive oil, the zucchini, bell pepper, garlic, and shallots.
7. Cook for 1 minute, then add the tomato and spicy V8 juices. Bring to a boil on medium-high heat. Reduce the heat to medium-low and bring to a simmer.
8. Return the mahi-mahi to the pan and coat with sauce. Cook for 5 to 7 minutes, or until the sauce thickens and reduces by half and the fish is tender.

The Build

Place a heaping scoop of cou cou in the center of a plate, and set a fish fillet and vegetables over the cou cou. Spoon sauce over all. Garnish with watercress. Plate the remaining servings and serve the Bajan hot sauce alongside.

SEAFOOD BOILS

CHEF KENNY'S CLASSIC SOUTHERN SEAFOOD BOIL

Garlic seafood boil with local shrimp, Dungeness crab legs,
crawfish, andouille sausage, potato, corn on the cob, and boiled eggs

202

KOREAN-INSPIRED SHELLFISH BOIL

Kimchi-garlic broth with shrimp, snow crab, scallops, crawfish, whole
garlic, Korean rice dumplings, baby bok choy, and baby corn

206

ITALIAN-INSPIRED SEAFOOD BOIL

Spicy tomato broth with clams, mussels, branzino, Italian sausage,
baby bell peppers, fingerling potatoes, and broccoli rabe

210

THAI CURRY SEAFOOD BOIL

Panang curry broth with green-lipped mussels, shrimp,
tilapia, Thai basil, Chinese sausage, new potatoes,
Thai eggplant, scallions, and duck eggs

214

FRENCH SEAFOOD BOIL

Pernod fennel broth with escargot, lobster, turbot, Parma ham,
baby zucchini, turnips, fingerling potatoes, and fennel pollen

218

In Jacksonville, Florida, there are restaurants and little shacks throughout the city that are known for seafood boils that feature garlic crabs. In the Black community, it is almost like a rite of passage to find the place that uses the right amount of garlic and butter to your liking. They are usually little holes-in-the-wall each with their own style of seafood boil.

My wife, Anna, is native to the Springfield area of Jacksonville, and seafood boils were a part of her food culture growing up. She is a pro when it comes to eating seafood, no crab or seafood crackers needed—she digs in all hands and teeth. When we first started dating, we hosted a get-together at her apartment. It was my first time meeting many of her friends and family members. I made a seafood boil that was spicy and flavorful. We had a great time playing cards, drinking, and laughing all night long. Whenever I make a boil, Anna gives the final blessing on it—just like my dad asked for my mom's final okay on his barbecue.

Both garlic crabs and Low Country seafood boil have their roots in Gullah Geechee culture. The Gullah Geechee are descendants of enslaved West Africans who lived in the coastal areas of the southeastern United States. Their recipes were passed down from generation to generation. I remember crabbing with my grandmother, who lived in St. Augustine, Florida. She would use spoiled chicken legs as bait and a cut milk jug on a rope as a trap—a crab could crawl in but couldn't get out—or we would simply tie a rope on the end of the chicken leg and throw it nearest the crab we could see. Once the crab got hold of the leg, we would gently pull the rope to shore, where we would scoop up the crab with a net. We were not always successful, but as a kid I had a lot of fun trying.

Every coastal community in the world has some sort of seafood boil–like dish made from what is available in that region. In the United States, from Baltimore to New Orleans, different communities have variations of seafood boil depending on what is plentiful. In Baltimore, blue crabs are featured; in New Orleans it's crawfish. If you live near the ocean, there are two things you can bank on always having on hand—seafood and water. Whether it's served with a six-pack of cold beer or a chilled bottle of white wine, a steaming pot of well-seasoned seafood is a crowd-pleaser no matter where you live.

Chef Kenny's Classic Southern Seafood Boil

When cooking a seafood boil for six people, you want a good tray of seafood: two crabs, six crawfish, six shrimp, plus sausage, potatoes, an ear of corn, and a few boiled eggs per person. It takes a big stockpot to make, with each element adding its flavor to the broth in stages. I start with the potatoes to make sure they have time to become tender, then the sausage so it adds its flavor, then the corn, crabs, and finally the shrimp and crawfish. I recommend investing in a large 3- to 5-gallon seafood stockpot if you want to cook a boil for a large party. There is nothing like a big spread of newspaper piled high with piping-hot Low Country boil as a dinner party centerpiece.

SERVES 6

INGREDIENTS

FOR THE BOIL BROTH
2 pounds garlic heads, cloves separated
    and peeled
1½ gallons water plus 1 cup for pureeing
    the garlic and onions
2 medium Spanish onions, quartered
2 pints lager
Juice of 8 to 10 navel oranges (2 cups)
Juice of 14 to 16 lemons (2 cups)
Juice of 14 to 16 limes (2 cups)
1 cup Chef Kenny's Raging Cajun Spice, or
    other Cajun seasoning
½ cup Chef Kenny's Fried Chicken Seasoning,
    or other poultry seasoning
1 cup granulated shrimp base, preferably
    Knorr shrimp bouillon
2 cups low-sodium soy sauce
½ cup fish sauce, preferably Viet Huong
    Three Crabs

FOR THE FINISHING BUTTER
1 pound (4 sticks) salted butter
Juice of 2 lemons (¼ cup)
Juice of 2 or 3 limes (¼ cup)
¼ cup low-sodium soy sauce
10 cloves garlic, peeled (¼ cup)
¼ medium yellow or white onion, cut into
    medium dice (¼ cup)
¼ cup Chef Kenny's Raging Cajun Spice, or
    other Cajun seasoning
2 tablespoons Chef Kenny's Fried Chicken
    Seasoning, or other poultry seasoning
¼ teaspoon xanthan gum

FOR THE BOIL
Boil Broth (see above)
12 new potatoes
6 ears corn, shucked
6 andouille sausage links
12 large eggs
6 clusters Dungeness crab
36 large fresh shrimp, head on
36 fresh crawfish

FOR THE BUILD
Chef Kenny's Raging Cajun Spice, or other
    Cajun seasoning

Make the Boil Broth

1. To prepare the ground garlic and onion, put the garlic cloves in a blender with ½ cup water. Puree until smooth (you should have 2 cups ground garlic). Transfer to a 3- to 5-gallon stockpot. Repeat with the onions, adding ½ cup water and pureeing in the blender until smooth, to make 2 cups ground onion. Transfer to the stockpot.
2. Add the 1½ gallons water, beer, citrus juices, Cajun and chicken seasonings, shrimp base, soy sauce, and fish sauce to the stockpot and bring to a boil on high heat.
3. Reduce the heat to medium and simmer for 10 minutes, until very fragrant and reddish in color. Keep warm over low heat.

Make the Finishing Butter

1. In a medium saucepan, combine the butter, citrus juices, soy sauce, garlic, onion, Cajun and chicken seasonings, and xanthan gum. Cook on medium heat for 10 minutes, until the butter is melted.
2. Puree with a handheld stick blender in the pot until smooth and emulsified. Cover to keep warm.

Make the Boil

1. Bring the broth to a simmer on medium heat.
2. Add the potatoes and cook for 20 minutes. Add the corn and sausage and cook for 10 minutes. Gently place the eggs in the broth and cook for 10 minutes. Use a long-handled strainer or spider to transfer the potatoes, corn, sausage, and eggs to serving bowls. Cover with foil to keep warm.
3. Bring the broth back to a boil.
4. Add the crabs to the broth and cook for 15 minutes. Add the shrimp and crawfish and cook for 8 minutes. Use the long-handled strainer to transfer the crabs, shrimp, and crawfish to individual serving bowls or platters. Cover with foil to keep warm.

The Build

1. Cover a table with newspaper or banana leaves. Arrange the potatoes, corn, sausage, and eggs on the paper, then add the seafood.
2. Place ramekins of the finishing butter around the table. Sprinkle Cajun seasoning over all components.

Korean-Inspired Shellfish Boil

The first time I had an Asian-style seafood boil was at a Korean hotpot restaurant. Similar to the garlic crab restaurants, Asian hotpot restaurants are places that feature seafood boils, only you get to cook the food at the table. Each one of these restaurants has their own spin; for example, I know a Vietnamese family who came to Florida by way of Louisiana, so crawfish is a main feature on their restaurant's hotpot menu. You can order one of their specialty boil bags, or you can customize it. They provide different types of broth, based on spice and flavor, to choose from. Korean hotpot is my favorite, but any hotpot restaurant is a great way to explore Asian flavors.

SERVES 6

FOR THE BOIL BROTH
2 pounds garlic heads, cloves separated and peeled
1½ gallons water plus 1 cup for pureeing the garlic and onions
2 medium yellow or white onions, quartered
2 pints sake
Juice of 8 to 10 navel oranges (2 cups)
Juice of 14 to 16 lemons (2 cups)
Juice of 14 to 16 limes (2 cups)
2 cups low-sodium soy sauce
1½ cups store-bought kimchi base
½ cup fish sauce, preferably Viet Huong Three Crabs
1 (4- to 5-inch) piece fresh ginger, peeled and grated (½ cup)
1 (6-inch) piece kombu (dried seaweed)
1 cup granulated shrimp base, preferably Knorr shrimp bouillon

FOR THE FINISHING BUTTER
1 pound (4 sticks) salted butter
Juice of 2 lemons (¼ cup)
Juice of 2 or 3 limes (¼ cup)
¼ cup low-sodium soy sauce
10 cloves garlic, peeled (¼ cup)
¼ small Spanish onion, cut into medium dice (¼ cup)
¼ cup store-bought kimchi base
1 (4-inch) piece fresh ginger, peeled and minced (¼ cup)
¼ teaspoon xanthan gum

FOR THE BOIL
6 heads garlic
18 ears canned baby corn
3 cups Korean rice cakes, preferably Sekero Rice Cake (Rice Ovalettes), rinsed
6 baby bok choy, halved
36 large fresh shrimp, head on
6 snow crab claw clusters
72 whole crawfish
18 (10/20-count) fresh scallops

FOR THE BUILD
¼ cup toasted sesame seeds
1 bunch cilantro, leaves only (1 cup)
4 limes, cut into wedges

Make the Boil Broth

1. To prepare the ground garlic and onion, put the garlic cloves in a blender with ½ cup water. Puree until smooth (you should have 2 cups ground garlic). Transfer to a 3- to 5-gallon stockpot. Repeat with the onions, adding ½ cup water and pureeing in the blender until smooth, to make 2 cups ground onion. Transfer to the stockpot.
2. Add the 1½ gallons water, sake, citrus juices, soy sauce, kimchi base, fish sauce, ginger, kombu, and shrimp base to the stockpot. Bring to a boil on high heat.
3. Reduce the heat to medium and simmer for 10 minutes, until very fragrant. Keep warm over low heat.

Make the Finishing Butter

1. In a medium saucepan, combine the butter, citrus juices, soy sauce, garlic, onion, kimchi base, ginger, and xanthan gum. Cook on medium heat for 10 minutes, until the butter is melted.
2. Puree with a handheld stick blender until smooth and emulsified. Cover to keep warm.

Make the Boil

1. Bring the boil broth to a simmer on medium heat.
2. Add the whole heads of garlic to the broth and cook for 20 minutes. Add the baby corn and rice cakes and cook for 5 minutes. Add the bok choy and cook for 2 minutes.
3. Use a long-handled strainer or spider to transfer the garlic, baby corn, rice cakes, and bok choy to serving bowls. Cover with foil to keep warm.
4. Bring the broth to a boil. Add the shrimp and cook for 8 minutes. Add the crab claw clusters and crawfish and cook for 5 minutes. Add the scallops and cook for 2 minutes. Use the long-handled strainer to transfer the shrimp, crab clusters, crawfish, and scallops to serving bowls or platters. Cover with foil to keep warm.

The Build

1. Place 1 head of garlic, 3 baby corn, 2 halves of baby bok choy, ½ cup rice cakes, 1 cluster of crab, 6 shrimp, 12 crawfish, and 3 scallops in a large bowl. Top each bowl with broth to keep moist.
2. Plate the remaining servings. Garnish with sesame seeds, fresh cilantro, and lime wedges. Place ramekins of finishing butter on the side for dipping. Let guests know they should squeeze out the garlic cloves.

Italian-Inspired Seafood Boil

This recipe is inspired by Italian cioppino, featuring traditional ingredients like tomato, garlic, peppers, and fresh citrus juice. In trying different versions of seafood boil from different regions to perfect my own original recipe, I attempted to dissect each one's unique flavors and build on them. Unlike traditional cioppino, I use soy sauce in all my boils to add a little umami pop to the dish. I look at it like *that's my salt.* I've found that soy sauce dissipates into the broth and provides just a little extra richness to the broth without overpowering the seafood—and in this dish it adds additional depth to the bright Italian flavors.

SERVES 6

FOR THE BOIL BROTH

2 pounds garlic heads, cloves separated
    and peeled
1 gallon water plus 1 cup for pureeing the
    garlic and onions
2 medium yellow or white onions, quartered
4 cups spicy V8 Juice
1 liter pinot grigio
2 cups low-sodium soy sauce
Juice of 14 to 16 lemons (2 cups)
2 (28-ounce) cans crushed tomatoes
1 (16-ounce) jar roasted red peppers,
    minced (2 cups)
1 cup granulated shrimp base, preferably Knorr
    shrimp bouillon
¼ cup crushed red pepper

FOR THE FINISHING BUTTER

1 pound (4 sticks) salted butter
Juice of 2 lemons (¼ cup)
Juice of 2 or 3 limes (¼ cup)
¼ cup low-sodium soy sauce
10 cloves garlic (¼ cup)
¼ medium yellow or white onion, cut into
    medium dice (¼ cup)
¼ cup jarred roasted red peppers
¼ bunch basil, leaves only (¼ cup)
¼ bunch flat-leaf parsley, leaves chopped (¼ cup)
1 tablespoon crushed red pepper
¼ teaspoon xanthan gum

FOR THE BOIL AND GARNISH

Boil Broth (see left)
12 fingerling potatoes or baby potatoes
6 Italian sausage links
12 baby bell peppers
1 bunch broccoli rabe
3 whole branzino, scaled, gutted, and
    cut in half, or 3 pounds branzino fillets,
    cut into 3-inch pieces
36 littleneck clams
36 rope-cultured mussels

FOR THE BUILD

1 bunch basil, leaves only (1 cup)
4 lemons, cut into wedges
Extra-virgin olive oil

Make the Boil Broth

1. To prepare the ground garlic and onion, put the garlic cloves in a blender with ½ cup water. Puree until smooth (you should have 2 cups ground garlic). Transfer to a 3- to 5-gallon stockpot. Repeat with the onions, adding ½ cup water and pureeing in the blender until smooth, to make 2 cups ground onion. Transfer to the stockpot.
2. Add the 1 gallon water, V8 juice, pinot grigio, soy sauce, lemon juice, crushed tomatoes, roasted red peppers, shrimp base, and crushed red pepper to the stockpot. Bring to a boil on high heat.
3. Reduce the heat to medium and simmer for 10 minutes, until very fragrant. Keep warm over low heat.

Make the Finishing Butter

1. In a medium saucepan, combine the butter, citrus juices, soy sauce, garlic, onion, roasted red peppers, basil, parsley, crushed red pepper, and xanthan gum. Cook on medium heat for 10 minutes, until the butter is melted.
2. Puree with a handheld stick blender until smooth and emulsified. Cover to keep warm.

Make the Boil

1. Bring the boil broth to a simmer on medium heat.
2. Add the potatoes and cook for 20 minutes. Add the sausage and baby bell peppers and cook for 10 minutes. Add the broccoli rabe and cook for 3 minutes. Use a long-handled strainer or spider to transfer the potatoes, sausage, baby bell peppers, and broccoli rabe to separate serving bowls. Cover with foil to keep warm.
3. Bring the broth back to a boil.
4. Add the branzino to the broth and cook for 15 minutes; if using fillets, cook for 5 minutes, or to desired doneness. Use the long-handled strainer or spider to transfer the branzino to a large bowl. Cover with foil to keep warm.
5. Add the clams and cook for 2 to 3 minutes, until the clams begin to open. Transfer the clams to another large bowl; discard any clams that don't open. Cover with foil to keep warm.
6. Cook the mussels for 2 minutes, until the mussels begin to open. Transfer the mussels to another bowl; discard any mussels that don't open. Cover with foil to keep warm.

The Build

Serve all the items individually in their own bowls and top each with boil broth to keep moist. Garnish each bowl with fresh basil leaves and lemon wedges. Drizzle a little extra-virgin olive over each component. Place the finishing butter in ramekins around the table.

Thai Curry Seafood Boil

Panang curry paste is a red curry paste with ground shrimp. When you cook the paste with herbs and other ingredients it comes together in a beautiful coconut-curry broth. You can use any type of seafood you would like with it. It is one of those curries that I crave whenever Thai cuisine is on my mind. This recipe calls for a heavy use of Golden Mountain Boy sauce. It is common in Thai cuisine and has a somewhat different flavor than traditional soy—its seasoning is a little lighter. It is a good condiment to have in the pantry.

SERVES 6

INGREDIENTS

FOR THE BOIL BROTH

2 pounds garlic heads, cloves separated and peeled

4 cups water plus 1 cup for pureeing the garlic and onions

2 medium yellow or white onions, quartered

128 ounces (1 gallon) canned coconut milk, preferably Thai Kitchen

2 pints sake

Juice of 14 to 16 lemons (2 cups)

Juice of 14 to 16 limes (2 cups)

1¼ cups Panang curry paste

1 cup Golden Mountain Boy Seasoning Sauce

1 cup granulated shrimp base, preferably Knorr shrimp bouillon

½ cup fish sauce

½ cup grated fresh ginger

½ cup fresh lemongrass, sliced (½-inch pieces), or 2 tablespoons lemongrass paste, preferably Cambodian

¼ cup granulated sugar

6 kaffir lime leaves, fresh or dried

FOR THE FINISHING BUTTER

1 pound (4 sticks) salted butter

¼ cup coconut vinegar

Juice of 2 or 3 limes (¼ cup)

2 tablespoons Golden Mountain Boy Seasoning Sauce

10 cloves garlic, peeled (¼ cup)

¼ medium yellow or white onion, cut into medium dice (¼ cup)

2 tablespoons Panang curry paste

1 (2-inch) piece fresh ginger, peeled and minced (2 tablespoons)

¼ bunch fresh Thai basil leaves or sweet basil leaves (¼ loosely packed cup)

3 dried Makrut lime leaves

2 tablespoons granulated sugar

¼ teaspoon xanthan gum

FOR THE BOIL

Boil Broth (see above)

12 ounces sweet potatoes, scrubbed and cut into large wedges, or baby potatoes (3 cups)

18 Thai green eggplant or 1 globe eggplant, cut into 2-inch cubes

6 duck eggs or large chicken eggs

1 (14-ounce) package Chinese sausage, links halved (3 cups)

1 bunch scallions, cut into 1-inch pieces (3 cups)

4 tilapia, scaled, cleaned, and cut into thirds, or 6 tilapia fillets

36 fresh shrimp, heads on or off

36 green-lipped mussels or black mussels

FOR THE BUILD

4 limes, cut into wedges

Sliced red or green serrano chiles

1 bunch Thai basil (1 loosely packed cup)

214   SOUTHERN COOKING • GLOBAL FLAVORS

Make the Boil Broth

1. To prepare the ground garlic and onion, put the garlic cloves in a blender with ½ cup water. Puree until smooth (you should have 2 cups ground garlic). Transfer to a 3- to 5-gallon stockpot. Repeat with the onions, adding ½ cup water and pureeing in the blender until smooth, to make 2 cups ground onion. Transfer to the stockpot.
2. Add the 4 cups water, coconut milk, sake, citrus juices, curry paste, seasoning sauce, shrimp base, fish sauce, ginger, lemongrass, sugar, and lime leaves to the stockpot. Bring to a boil on high heat.
3. Reduce the heat to medium and simmer for 10 minutes, until very fragrant. Keep warm over low heat.

Make the Finishing Butter

1. In a medium saucepan, combine the butter, coconut vinegar, lime juice, seasoning sauce, garlic, onion, curry paste, ginger, basil, lime leaves, sugar, and xanthan gum. Cook on medium heat for 10 minutes, until the butter is melted.
2. Puree with a handheld stick blender in the pot until smooth and emulsified. Cover to keep warm.

Make the Boil

1. Bring the boil broth to a simmer on medium heat.
2. Add the sweet potatoes and Thai eggplant and cook for 15 minutes. Add the duck eggs and cook for 5 minutes. Add the Chinese sausage and cook for 3 minutes. Add the scallions and cook for 1 minute. Use a long-handled strainer or spider to transfer the potatoes, eggplant, eggs, sausage, and scallions to individual serving bowls. Cover with foil to keep warm.
3. Bring the broth to a boil.
4. Add the tilapia to the broth and cook for 15 minutes, or cook fillets for 3 to 5 minutes. Use the long-handled strainer or spider to transfer to a large bowl and cover with foil to keep warm. Add the shrimp and cook for 5 minutes. Transfer to a large bowl and cover with foil to keep warm. Cook the mussels for 2 minutes, until the mussels begin to open. Transfer the mussels to another bowl; discard any mussels that don't open. Cover with foil to keep warm.

The Build

Serve all the items individually in their own bowls and top each with boil broth to keep moist. Garnish with limes, sliced serrano chiles, and fresh Thai basil. Place ramekins of finishing butter on the side for dipping.

French Seafood Boil

I learned how to make classic bouillabaisse while working at the Ritz-Carlton. I knew I had nailed the bouillabaisse when French guests came into the kitchen after eating it to ask where to find the French chef who had made their meal. Bouillabaisse made in France tastes different than it does in any other part of the world, because of the minerals in the water and the soil. You can get close using key ingredients—Pernod, fennel, and a softer chile pepper like Espelette. It's all about a broth infused with fennel, anise, a little citrus, and spice that makes an elegant, simple boil.

SERVES 6

FOR THE BOIL BROTH

2 pounds garlic heads, cloves separated

1½ gallons water plus 1 cup for pureeing the garlic and onions

2 medium yellow or white onions, quartered

1 liter Pernod

Juice of 14 to 16 lemons (2 cups)

4 cups ground fresh fennel

¼ cup Espelette pepper

1 cup granulated shrimp base, preferably Knorr shrimp bouillon

FOR THE FINISHING BUTTER

1 pound (4 sticks) salted butter

Juice of 2 lemons (¼ cup)

Juice of 2 or 3 limes (¼ cup)

2 tablespoons low-sodium soy sauce

10 cloves garlic, peeled (¼ cup)

½ medium yellow or white onion, cut into medium dice (½ cup)

¼ cup medium-diced fennel

¼ cup fresh tarragon or flat-leaf parsley leaves

1 tablespoon Espelette pepper

¼ teaspoon xanthan gum

FOR THE BOIL

Boil Broth (see left)

12 fingerling potatoes or baby potatoes

12 baby turnips, or 3 medium turnips, cut into wedges

18 baby zucchini, or 4 standard zucchini, cut into 1-inch pieces

1 pound thinly sliced Parma ham

6 (1¼-pound) Maine lobsters or Caribbean lobster tails

36 large escargots, in or out of the shell

6 (4- to 5-ounce) skinless turbot or flounder fillets

FOR THE BUILD

Fresh tarragon leaves, for garnish

Lemon wedges, for garnish

Make the Boil Broth

1. To prepare the ground garlic and onion, put the garlic cloves in a blender with ½ cup water. Puree until smooth (you should have 2 cups ground garlic). Transfer to a 3- to 5-gallon stockpot. Repeat with the onions, adding ½ cup water and pureeing in the blender until smooth, to make 2 cups ground onion. Transfer to the stockpot.
2. Add the 1½ gallons water, Pernod, lemon juice, ground fennel, Espelette pepper, and shrimp base to the stockpot and bring to a boil on high heat.
3. Reduce the heat to medium and simmer for 10 minutes, until very fragrant. Keep warm over low heat.

Make the Finishing Butter

1. In a medium saucepan, combine the butter, citrus juices, soy sauce, garlic, onion, fennel, tarragon, Espelette pepper, and xanthan gum. Cook on medium heat for 10 minutes, until the butter is melted.
2. Puree with a handheld stick blender until smooth and emulsified. Cover to keep warm.

Make the Boil

1. Bring the boil broth to a simmer on medium heat.
2. Add the potatoes and cook for 20 minutes. Add the turnips and cook for 10 minutes. Add the zucchini and cook for 3 minutes. Add the Parma ham and cook for 1 minute. Use a long-handled strainer or spider to transfer the potatoes, turnips, zucchini, and ham to individual serving bowls. Cover with foil to keep warm.
3. Bring the broth back to a boil.
4. Add the lobster to the broth and cook for 10 minutes. Use the long-handled strainer or spider to transfer to a large bowl and cover with foil to keep warm.
5. Add the escargots and cook for 10 minutes. Transfer to a large bowl and cover with foil to keep warm.
6. Add the turbot and cook for 5 minutes. Transfer to a platter and and cover with foil to keep warm.

The Build

Serve all the items individually in their own dishes and top each with boil broth to stay moist. Garnish the bowls with tarragon and lemon wedges. Place ramekins of finishing butter on the side for dipping.

COLLARDS
+ CORN

BREAD

SLOW-COOKED CLASSIC COLLARD GREENS
AND SKILLET CORNBREAD

Collards cooked in "mother's milk" broth and served with buttermilk
skillet cornbread studded with cracklings, jalapeño, and fresh corn

228

THAI COLLARD GREEN SALAD AND
COCONUT CORNBREAD CREPES

Fresh collard green salad with dried shrimp, Thai chiles, and
peanuts, served with a coconut milk–cornbread crepe

232

COLLARD GREEN MINESTRONE AND
CORNBREAD PANZANELLA SALAD

Spicy Italian sausage and tomato broth with black-eyed peas,
vegetables, and collard greens topped with collard green pesto,
served with a cornbread panzanella salad

236

COLLARD GREEN KIMCHI SOUP WITH
CORNBREAD DUMPLINGS

Kimchi collard green stems and young collard greens simmered
with cornbread dumplings and grilled beef short ribs

240

COCONUT-CURRY COLLARD GREENS WITH
PINEAPPLE-CORNBREAD GREMOLATA

Coconut-curry collard greens with jerk-style pork chops and
a topping of pineapple-cornbread gremolata

244

A hot bowl of collard greens with a ham hock on top and a side of warm, buttered cornbread is like heaven to me. During the holidays when I was growing up, we always had collards and cornbread. Family would come from the Carolinas, Georgia, and Florida. My mom would always cook collards in a big old pot, then just leave them in the pot for people to serve themselves. Cornbread was always baked and served in a cast-iron skillet. She would cook two types of greens—collards with smoked ham hocks or bacon, and turnip and mustard greens with smoked turkey wings. We would all enjoy a little of both on the plate.

My mother taught me how to cook collards and cornbread. It is a simple process, but it takes four to six hours to cook greens properly. Collards are grown in sandy dirt, so they are very gritty. It is important to wash them well. My mom would fill the sink with water and then submerge the collards. The sand would settle at the bottom of the sink. She would repeat this process at least four or five times, until the bottom of the sink was clear of sand and dirt. Once clean, she would remove the leaves from the stems, then cut the leaves into one-inch pieces. Next, into a pot of water, but not too much, because the greens release water when cooking. They would cook down and she would add pork, onion, apple cider vinegar, a little sugar, and a pinch of crushed red pepper.

Enslaved Africans brought collard greens to America. They are sturdy leafy greens that grow quickly, and it is traditional to braise them to make them tender and easy to digest. Every Southern family has its own recipe, but I have always known a classic collard dish to be cooked with smoked ham hocks. Ham hocks are a scrap meat that enslaved people would salt cure to preserve. They were often used as a staple of one-pot meals cooked over a fire.

The smoked ham hock broth of a pot of collard greens is known as pot likker. In the American South, it is like the consommé of France or the pho broth of Vietnam. Like those classic broths, it is deeply rooted to the culture of the people who invented it. I was cooking in a kitchen in the Georgia Sea Islands when I first heard the term "mother's milk" used to describe pot likker. I worked with a man who was raised by a Black nanny, and she called pot likker mother's milk. I am not sure of the origins of the term—maybe it is from all the love our mothers put into making collards, or its history as a nutrient-rich tonic once prescribed by doctors for its health benefits—but what I do know is that, whatever you call it, a warm mug of pot likker seems like it would cure just about anything.

Slow-Cooked Classic Collard Greens and Skillet Cornbread

A cinnamon stick is the secret ingredient in my collards. Cinnamon is also a great addition to cornbread. My grandmother used to sprinkle a little cinnamon and sugar on top of her cornbread batter before baking it, just giving it a little extra sweetness. My first introduction to cornbread was a box of Jiffy corn muffin mix when I was a kid. I would add a little jalapeño to spice it up or maybe a little extra corn for texture. Try your own spin on it. One tip on the mother's milk is to make it overnight. You can put it on the stove over very low heat, and just let it go.

SERVES 6

FOR THE MOTHER'S MILK (SMOKED HAM HOCK STOCK)
2½ pounds smoked ham hocks
3 quarts water

FOR THE COLLARD GREENS
8 ounces salt pork, cut into small dice or ground
2½ to 3 quarts Mother's Milk (see above)
2 pounds cooked and chopped smoked ham hock meat (reserved from Mother's Milk)
1 cup apple cider vinegar
½ cup packed light brown sugar
2 cinnamon sticks
1 teaspoon crushed red pepper
2 large bunches collard greens (4 to 5 pounds total), leaves stemmed and chopped into 1-inch pieces
½ cup fried shallots, preferably Maesri
¼ cup fried garlic, preferably Maesri
1 tablespoon kosher salt

FOR THE SKILLET CORNBREAD
8 ounces salt pork, ground with a meat grinder, or cut into small dice
2 cups self-rising flour
2 cups cornmeal
2 cups fresh corn kernels (from about 2 ears)
1 (15-ounce) can creamed corn
¼ cup granulated sugar
1 jalapeño pepper, chopped
1 tablespoon kosher salt
1½ cups buttermilk
½ cup water
4 large eggs
½ cup (1 stick) salted butter, melted, plus 4 tablespoons (½ stick) for coating

**Make the
Mother's Milk**

1. Place the smoked ham hocks in a large stockpot. Add the water and bring to a boil on high heat. Reduce the heat to low and cover with a lid. Cook for 6 hours.
2. Strain the mother's milk through a fine-mesh strainer into another large stockpot.
3. Remove the bone from the hocks and chop up the meat and fat; transfer to the stockpot.

**Make the
Collard Greens**

1. Place the salt pork in a microwavable container and microwave on high for 3 minutes. Stir and microwave for another 3 minutes. The fat will render and the meat will become salty, crispy bits (cracklings).
2. Transfer the rendered fat and cracklings to the stockpot of mother's milk and ham hock meat. Add the apple cider vinegar, brown sugar, cinnamon sticks, and crushed red pepper.
3. Bring to a boil on high heat and add the collard greens. Stir thoroughly.
4. Cover with a lid, reduce the heat to low, and cook for 3 hours. The greens will darken and become tender.
5. Add the fried shallots, fried garlic, and salt and simmer for 1 hour, until the greens are very tender. Keep warm, covered, until ready to serve.

**Make the
Skillet Cornbread**

1. Preheat the oven to 400°F.
2. Place the salt pork in a microwavable container and microwave for 3 minutes. Stir and microwave for another 3 minutes.
3. Pour the rendered pork fat into a large cast-iron skillet. Reserve the cracklings.
4. Combine the flour, cornmeal, fresh corn kernels, creamed corn, sugar, jalapeño, reserved salt pork cracklings, and salt in a large bowl. Add the buttermilk, water, eggs, and melted butter. Mix until the batter is slightly smooth.
5. Place the cast-iron skillet in the oven and heat for 5 minutes.
6. Carefully remove the skillet from the oven and pour in the batter. Return the skillet to the oven and bake for 15 minutes.
7. Rotate the skillet and bake for another 9 minutes, or until the cornbread is golden brown and firm to the touch. A toothpick inserted into the center should come out clean.
8. Rub the top of the baked cornbread with the half stick of butter. Cool to room temperature.

The Build

Put a large helping of the greens into a bowl and serve with a wedge of cornbread. Plate the remaining servings.

Thai Collard Green Salad and Coconut Cornbread Crepes

Green papaya salad is the inspiration for this recipe. It is traditionally served with sticky rice and roasted chicken marinated in yellow curry cooked over hot coals. In this recipe, I swap the papaya for collards. Similar to how the acid from the lime and fish sauce breaks down the fibrous papaya, the acids here tenderize the collard greens. Collards are in the cabbage family, and can be used to make a crunchy slaw whose flavors are light and bright. To make a creamy version, just add a little sour cream or mayonnaise. The highlight of this dish is how the fresh sweet flavor of the collards comes through, and paired with the sweetness of the corn in the crepes, it is magical.

SERVES 6

INGREDIENTS

FOR THE COLLARD GREEN SALAD
¼ cup dried shrimp
½ cup coconut palm sugar
6 cloves garlic, peeled
2 Thai (bird) chiles, stemmed
½ pint red grape tomatoes
½ medium red bell pepper, cut into medium dice (½ cup)
1 tablespoon kosher salt
¼ cup fish sauce or Golden Mountain Boy Seasoning Sauce
Juice of 2 or 3 limes (¼ cup)
1 bunch collard greens, leaves stemmed and thinly sliced
½ cup roasted unsalted peanuts
½ bunch Thai basil or sweet basil, leaves only (½ cup)

FOR THE COCONUT CORNBREAD CREPES
½ cup self-rising flour
½ cup cornmeal
¼ cup granulated sugar
1 tablespoon ground ginger
1 teaspoon kosher salt
2 large eggs
1 cup canned coconut milk, preferably Thai Kitchen
¼ cup coconut oil

FOR THE BUILD
Crushed roasted peanuts, for garnish
Lime wedges, for garnish

Make the Collard Green Salad

1. Use a mortar and pestle or a food processor fitted with a metal blade to crush or finely mince the dried shrimp, palm sugar, garlic, and Thai chiles.
2. Add the grape tomatoes, bell pepper, and salt. Pound together gently or pulse in the food processor.
3. Pour in the fish sauce and lime juice. Mash together or pulse in the food processor.
4. Add the collard greens and pound gently to break up the fibers or briefly pulse in the food processor. Transfer to a large serving bowl.
5. Gently mix in the peanuts and Thai basil. Reserve until ready to serve.

Make the Coconut Cornbread Crepes

1. Heat a pancake griddle or nonstick skillet on medium.
2. Combine the self-rising flour, cornmeal, sugar, ginger, and salt in a medium bowl.
3. Add the eggs, coconut milk, and coconut oil to the flour mixture and mix thoroughly.
4. Put ¼ cup of the batter on the hot griddle. Cook for 1 minute, or until the top of the crepe has lots of bubbles.
5. Use a spatula to help you flip the crepe. Cook the other side for 30 seconds.
6. Transfer the crepe to a platter and cover with a kitchen towel. Repeat until all the batter is used. As the crepes finish cooking, stack them on top of one another and cover with the towel to keep warm until ready to serve.

The Build

Either roll the salad in the crepes or enjoy it alongside the crepes. Garnish with crushed roasted peanuts and lime wedges.

Collard Green Minestrone and Cornbread Panzanella Salad

I love taking authentic Southern greens and incorporating them into a pesto. I think it allows the flavor of the greens to become more pronounced. In this preparation, I added a little flat-leaf parsley and sage. Their flavors don't compete with collards but complement them. The pesto really kicks up the flavor in the minestrone a notch, adding a rich, herbaceous note to the soup. The addition of V8 juice does the same and is a great shortcut to making a delicious minestrone. Made from a variety of vegetables, it gives the soup a different depth of flavor.

FOR THE COLLARD GREEN PESTO
1 cup extra-virgin olive oil
5 cloves garlic, peeled
Juice of 2 lemons (¼ cup)
¼ cup pine nuts
¼ cup grated Parmesan cheese
¼ teaspoon kosher salt
4 to 5 sprigs sage, leaves only (½ cup)
½ bunch flat-leaf parsley leaves (½ cup)
1 small bunch collard greens, leaves stemmed
    and chopped (2 cups)

FOR THE MINESTRONE SOUP
½ cup mild olive oil
1 pound spicy Italian sausages,
    casings removed
¼ cup chopped garlic
1 medium yellow or white onion, cut into
    medium dice (1 cup)
5 ounces carrots, cut into medium dice (1 cup)
4 medium ribs celery, cut into medium dice
    (1 cup)
1 medium red bell pepper, cut into medium dice
    (1 cup)
8 cups (1 quart) V8 juice

4 cups low-sodium chicken stock
1 cup canned diced tomatoes
    (from a 14-ounce can)
1 medium bunch collard greens, stemmed and
    coarsely chopped (3 cups)
1 cup drained canned black-eyed peas
    (from a 15-ounce can)
½ cup cooked ditalini pasta
¼ bunch flat-leaf parsley, leaves chopped (¼ cup)
Kosher salt and freshly ground black pepper

FOR THE PANZANELLA SALAD
Skillet Cornbread (see page 228), cubed (3 cups)
1 cup extra-virgin olive oil
½ medium red onion, cut into small dice (½ cup)
½ medium red bell pepper, cut into small dice
    (½ cup)
½ cup small-diced fennel
¼ cup chopped garlic
½ cup white balsamic vinegar
¼ cup honey
1 or 2 stemmed collard green leaves,
    cut into thin ribbons (1 cup)
1 bunch basil, leaves only (1 cup)
3½ ounces Parmesan cheese, grated (1 cup)

Make the Collard Green Pesto

1. Put the olive oil, garlic, lemon juice, pine nuts, Parmesan, and salt in a blender and puree until smooth.
2. Add the sage, parsley, and collard greens and blend until smooth.
3. Transfer to a bowl and reserve. (The pesto can be made up to 3 days in advance and stored in an airtight container in the fridge.)

Make the Minestrone Soup

1. Put the olive oil and Italian sausages in a large stockpot on medium heat. Break up the sausage and cook until browned, about 10 minutes.
2. Add the garlic, onion, carrot, celery, and bell pepper and sweat for 2 minutes. Pour in the V8 juice, stock, and canned tomatoes. Bring to a boil over high heat, then simmer on medium-low heat.
3. Stir in the collard greens. Cover the pot and cook for 30 minutes. Add the black-eyed peas, pasta, and parsley. Cook for 5 minutes. Season with salt and black pepper to taste. Keep warm on low heat.

Make the Panzanella Salad

1. Preheat the oven to 400°F.
2. Put the cornbread cubes on a sheet pan and toast in the oven for 10 minutes. Toss the cornbread pieces, rotate the pan, and toast for another 5 minutes, until lightly browned.
3. Warm a large skillet on medium heat and add the olive oil. Sauté the onion, bell pepper, fennel, and garlic until slightly browned.
4. Reduce the heat to low and add the toasted cornbread. Gently toss together.
5. Whisk the balsamic vinegar and honey in a small bowl and add it to the skillet with the cornbread and vegetables. Fold in the basil and collard greens.
6. Transfer the salad to a large serving bowl and garnish with some of the Parmesan cheese.

The Build

Serve family style. Set the pot of soup and the salad on the table. Garnish bowls of soup with the pesto and Parmesan cheese and serve the salad in bowls or on plates.

Collard Green Kimchi Soup with Cornmeal Dumplings

Kimchi is an essential Korean food, and it is served on every Korean table. Many families make their kimchi from scratch using fermented chiles, but another option is to buy kimchi base. You can get this in most Asian markets or online. It is so easy—take some chopped cabbage, toss it in the kimchi base, and let it do its thing. Even better: The Kimchi can be made up to one week ahead. The cornmeal dumplings that go in the soup are a signature dish from a small coastal town near St. Mary's, Georgia. They would use the pot likker with a little bit of greens as a broth to cook the cornbread dumplings. Korean kimchi soup is usually made with rice dumplings; the cornmeal dumplings give a uniquely Southern spin on an Asian classic.

SERVES 6

FOR THE COLLARD GREEN KIMCHI

1 bunch collard greens, stems only, cut into
    1-inch pieces (4 cups); reserve the leaves
    for the soup
½ cup peeled garlic cloves
¾ cup store-bought kimchi base

FOR THE CORNMEAL DUMPLINGS

2 russet potatoes
1 cup self-rising flour
1 cup cornmeal
1 tablespoon ground ginger
1 teaspoon kosher salt
2 large eggs
4 tablespoon (½ stick) salted butter, melted
1 cup semolina flour, for dusting
Kosher salt
¼ cup canola or corn oil

FOR THE SOUP

2 pounds Korean-cut beef short ribs,
    or New York strip, flank, skirt,
    or hanger steak
½ cup low-sodium soy sauce
¼ cup sesame oil
1 tablespoon kosher salt
1 tablespoon freshly ground black pepper
Vegetable oil, for frying (optional)
8 cups low-sodium chicken stock
Collard Green Kimchi (see above)
½ cup store-bought kimchi base
2 to 4 stemmed collard green leaves, cut into
    thin ribbons (2 cups)
1 medium carrot, cut into medium dice (½ cup)
½ turnip, cut into large dice (½ cup)
½ medium red bell pepper, cut into medium
    dice (½ cup)
3 cups cooked Cornmeal Dumplings (see left,
    page 242)

| **Make the Collard Green Kimchi** | Combine the collard green stems, garlic, and kimchi base in a medium bowl. Transfer to a 1-gallon freezer bag and seal, being sure to squeeze out all the air. Set in the refrigerator for 24 hours or up to 1 week. |

Make the Dumplings

1. Put the potatoes in a large pot and cover with cold water. Bring to a boil, covered, on medium-high heat.
2. Reduce the heat to medium-low and simmer for 25 to 30 minutes, or until the potatoes are fork-tender.
3. Drain the potatoes. Put the potatoes between layers of paper towel—the potatoes will be hot—and carefully peel away the skins. Set aside the potato flesh.
4. Sift together the self-rising flour, cornmeal, ginger, and salt into a medium bowl. Put the flour mixture on a clean counter.
5. Rice the potatoes over the flour mixture. Alternatively, grate on a box grater and add to the flour. Use a dough scraper to combine, or cut, the hot potatoes into the flour mixture.
6. Add the eggs and melted butter to the potato-flour dough, and continue to gently cut and scrape the dough until it becomes smooth.
7. Cover with a clean kitchen towel and let the dough rest for 5 minutes. Line a sheet pan with parchment paper and dust with semolina flour.
8. Lightly dust the counter with some of the semolina flour. Place the dough on the floured surface and cut it into 4 equal pieces.
9. With your hands, roll one piece of dough into a rope about 12 inches long and ½ inch wide. Cut the rope into 1-inch pieces and lightly dust with semolina flour.
10. Gently scoop up the dumplings and place them on the prepared sheet pan. Repeat with the other pieces of dough.
11. Transfer the sheet pan to the refrigerator and chill the dumplings for 15 minutes.
12. Bring a large pot of salted water to boil. Prepare a bowl with ice and cold water.
13. Cook the dumplings in small batches, gently stirring them while they cook. Once the dumplings begin to float, cook them for an additional 2 minutes.
14. Use a long-handled strainer or spider to transfer the dumplings to the ice bath. Allow them to become cool to the touch, about 2 minutes.
15. Remove from the ice bath, put in a bowl, and toss with the oil to prevent sticking. Reserve.

Make the Soup

1. Preheat a charcoal or gas grill to medium-high. Alternatively, the short ribs can be cooked on the stovetop.
2. Combine the short ribs, soy sauce, sesame oil, salt, and black pepper in a 1-gallon resealable plastic bag. Seal the bag and squeeze it to coat the ribs.
3. Marinate the ribs for a minimum of 30 minutes at room temperature or up to 24 hours in the refrigerator.

4. If cooking the ribs on the stovetop, heat a cast-iron skillet on medium-high with a bit of oil. Remove the ribs from the marinade and grill or cook for 3 minutes per side. Set aside.

5. Combine the stock, collard green kimchi, kimchi base, and garlic in a large pot and bring to a boil over high heat. Reduce the heat to medium-low and simmer for 10 minutes.

6. Add the grilled ribs and cook for 10 minutes. Add the collard greens, carrot, turnip, bell pepper, and dumplings and cook for 5 minutes.

The Build   Serve family style. Set the pot of soup on the table with bowls and spoons, and dig in.

Coconut-Curry Collard Greens with Pineapple-Cornbread Gremolata

This dish has a little bit of everything from everywhere. In the Caribbean, due to the Indian influence, a lot of the curries that are enjoyed there are yellow Madras-style curries. The collard greens cooked in coconut curry are reminiscent of Indian saag paneer, which is creamy and made with spinach. Gremolata is a classic Italian green garnish, featuring breadcrumbs, a fresh green herb, garlic, and olive oil. In my version, the acidity of the pickled pineapple combined with the onion and cilantro pairs wonderfully with the sweetness of the cornbread.

SERVES 6

INGREDIENTS

FOR CHEF KENNY'S CURRY STARTER
Makes 6 cups

4 ounces fresh ginger, peeled and sliced (1 cup)

1 cup peeled garlic cloves

1 small Spanish onion, sliced (1 cup)

½ cup water

1 cup ghee or clarified butter

FOR THE COCONUT-CURRY COLLARD GREENS

1 large bunch collard greens, leaves stemmed and coarsely chopped (10 cups)

1 cup Chef Kenny's Curry Starter

½ cup vegetable oil

½ cup Madras yellow curry powder

1 small Spanish onion, cut into small dice (1 cup)

1 habanero pepper, chopped

4 cups canned coconut milk, preferably Thai Kitchen

¼ cup low-sodium soy sauce

Juice of 2 or 3 limes (¼ cup)

¼ cup granulated sugar

FOR THE PINEAPPLE-CORNBREAD GREMOLATA

1 cup crumbled Skillet Cornbread (see page 228)

½ cup canned crushed pineapple

¼ medium yellow or white onion, minced (¼ cup)

2 tablespoons minced garlic (about 4 cloves)

1 bunch flat-leaf parsley, leaves chopped (1 cup)

½ bunch cilantro, chopped (½ cup)

Juice of 1 lime

Kosher salt

FOR THE PORK CHOPS

1 cup vegetable oil, plus more if needed

½ cup Chef Kenny's Jerk Spice, or other jerk seasoning

½ small Spanish onion, cut into large dice (½ cup)

½ medium green bell pepper, cut into large dice (½ cup)

¼ bunch flat-leaf parsley leaves (¼ cup)

¼ bunch marjoram or oregano leaves (¼ cup)

5 cloves garlic, peeled

1 habanero pepper, stemmed

½ cup spiced rum

6 (6-ounce) pork chops, bone-in

FOR THE BUILD

6 grilled limes (see page 95)

Make Chef Kenny's Curry Starter

1. Put the ginger, garlic, onion, and water into a blender and purée until smooth. Transfer the pureed vegetables to a medium saucepan and add the ghee. Stir to combine over medium-high heat.
2. Bring to a boil, then reduce the heat to low and simmer for 20 minutes.
3. Allow the curry starter to cool, then place in an airtight container and refrigerate. (The curry starter can be made ahead and stored in the refrigerator up to 30 days.)

Make the Coconut-Curry Collard Greens

1. Boil the collard greens in a large pot of water on medium-high heat. Reduce the heat to medium-low and simmer for 1 hour. Drain the greens and reserve.
2. To the pot, add the curry starter, vegetable oil, curry powder, onion, and habanero. Cook on medium heat for 2 to 3 minutes, stirring often.
3. Add the coconut milk, soy sauce, lime juice, and sugar and bring to a simmer.
4. Return the collard greens to the pot and bring to a simmer on medium-low heat. Cook for 30 minutes. Remove from the heat and cover to keep warm.

Make the Pineapple-Cornbread Gremolata

1. Preheat the oven to 350°F.
2. Put the cornbread crumbles on a small sheet pan and toast for about 10 minutes. Stir the crumbles and toast for another 5 minutes, until golden brown. Transfer the crumbles to a medium bowl and allow to cool.
3. Add the pineapple, onion, garlic, parsley, cilantro, lime juice, and salt to the bowl with the cornbread crumbles. Gently toss together. Reserve until ready to serve.

Make the Pork Chops

1. Put the oil, jerk seasoning, onion, bell pepper, parsley, marjoram, garlic, habanero, and spiced rum into a blender and puree until smooth. Transfer the marinade to a 1-gallon resealable plastic bag. Add the pork chops to the bag with the marinade. Seal the bag and squeeze it to coat the pork chops. Marinate for a minimum of 1 hour at room temperature and up to 8 hours in the refrigerator.
2. If you marinated the pork chops in the fridge, pull them out and allow to come to room temperature, about 30 to 45 minutes.
3. Preheat a gas or charcoal grill to medium-high. If you're not using a grill, heat a cast-iron skillet over high heat with a little oil.
4. Grill or cook the pork chops 4 to 5 minutes per side, or until a meat thermometer inserted into the center of a pork chop registers 145° to 155°F. Rest 10 minutes before serving.

The Build

Place a heaping spoonful of curried collard greens in the center of a plate. Top the greens with a pork chop. Garnish the pork chop with the pineapple-cornbread gremolata and add a charred lime. Plate the remaining servings.

CAKES
+ PIES

FLORIDA CITRUS CAKE

A moist lemon-vanilla cake with citrus cream cheese frosting
and blackberries

254

SPANISH HOT CHOCOLATE CAKE

A rich, bold-flavored chocolate cake topped with
toasted marshmallows and blood orange

258

GUAVA DUFF CAKE

A bright, fruit-forward cake with Coconut Guava Frosting,
toasted coconut, and macerated pineapple

262

DELLA'S SWEET POTATO PIE

A custardy sweet potato pie with vanilla buttermilk sauce and blackberries

266

CHOCOLATE-BOURBON PECAN PIE

A Southern classic with chocolate and nutty undertones,
dusted with powdered sugar

270

STRAWBERRY-ROSEMARY COBBLER PIE

A light berry and citrus pie with limoncello–black pepper Chantilly

274

Baking is all about paying attention to the details—there's no eyeballing. I love the exactness of it because it really makes me slow down to properly execute. Baking reminds me of family time, of being young and spending quality time with my parents. My parents made food a focus in our lives growing up, and cooking was an experience that we shared together.

My mom used to take me to the grocery store, and I was allowed to buy a few ingredients to play around with. My mom was big into seasoning. She would let me buy new seasonings to try, but the rule was that whatever I bought I had to eat. I learned quickly what was good and what wasn't good when you were baking. I baked from *The Betty Crocker Cookbook*. My mom would have me break down ingredient measurements and use them to learn about math and fractions. I took notes in the book, playing around with different recipes and adding my own spin. I would add spices or new ingredients like fruit. We had a lot of wild berries that grew throughout the Cleveland area, and when we would go hiking, I would collect them and bring them home to bake with. Berries, citrus, and spices. These are the three things I enjoy most in desserts, and this is why I often feature these ingredients when baking.

Della, my grandmother—a diabetic with a sweet tooth—also baked a lot. I remember walking into her home in St. Augustine, Florida—it always smelled like delicious food cooking. She would bake for others, her family, and extended family. She loved sweet potato pie and would make little sweet potato turnovers for us with the leftover pie dough and filling.

Pie is seasonal, at least to my way of thinking. It is something I crave in the fall and winter and makes me nostalgic for holidays as a kid. While lots of people think cakes are for special occasions, they can be for anytime.

No matter what time of year or occasion, dessert is a treat, and treats are best shared. The recipes in this chapter make more than one cake or pie. Even though it's a little unusual, I did this on purpose: I encourage you to bake not just for yourself, but for friends or family members who may need something sweet to brighten their day. There is nothing better than receiving an unexpected dessert from someone who cares. It is a small act of love and a way to make life better. Nothing says "love" like a warm pie or decadent cake.

Florida Citrus Cake

The first cake I ever had was a lemon sour cream pound cake. It is my mom's specialty cake, and she would make it all the time. As a kid, I remember loving the lemon sour cream icing she poured over the moist, buttery cake. My mom instilled in me early on an appreciation for the combination of sweet a nd sour in desserts, which I still carry with me today.

MAKES SIX (6-INCH) CAKES OR THREE (9-INCH) CAKES

FOR THE CITRUS SUGAR
1 cup granulated sugar
Peel from 1 orange (reserve the fruit)
Peel from 1 lime (reserve the fruit)
Peel from 1 lemon (reserve the fruit)

FOR THE CAKE
Makes 6½ to 7 cups batter

Butter or pan spray, for greasing
3 cups self-rising flour
2 cups granulated sugar
½ teaspoon kosher salt
1 teaspoon xanthan gum
2 cups buttermilk
¼ cup vegetable oil
Juice of 4 lemons (½ cup)
Juice of 4 or 5 limes (½ cup)
Juice of 2 navel oranges (½ cup)
2 large eggs
¼ cup sour cream
1 tablespoon vanilla bean paste or
    vanilla extract

FOR THE FROSTING
½ cup (1 stick) salted butter, softened
4 ounces vegetable shortening (½ cup)
1 (8-ounce) block cream cheese
1 pound powdered sugar
1 tablespoon lemon extract

FOR THE BUILD
Blackberries, for garnish
Powdered sugar, for dusting

Make the Citrus Sugar

1. Put the sugar and citrus peels in a food processor fitted with the metal blade. Process until the citrus peels are thoroughly incorporated into the sugar.
2. Transfer to a freezer-safe container or freezer bag. Freeze until ready to use, or up to 6 months.

Make the Cake

1. Preheat the oven to 325°F. Grease your pans of choice.
2. Combine the flour, sugar, salt, and xanthan gum in a large bowl.
3. Add the buttermilk, vegetable oil, citrus juices, eggs, sour cream, and vanilla bean paste to the flour mixture. Whisk thoroughly.
4. Divide the batter among the pans and place the pans on a sheet pan. (The sheet pan makes transitioning the batter-filled pans to the oven easier, avoiding spills.)
5. Bake the cakes for 7 minutes. Rotate the sheet pan and bake for another 7 minutes, or until the cakes are golden brown, springy to the touch, and a toothpick inserted into the center of each cake comes out clean.
6. Let the cakes cool to room temperature. Once cool, remove the cakes from the pans. Place a serving plate/platter over a pan. Turn the plate over while holding the pan. Gently free the cake pan from the cake and place on a wire rack. Repeat for the remaining cakes.

Make the Frosting

1. In the bowl of a stand mixer with the paddle attachment, mix the butter, shortening, cream cheese, powdered sugar, and lemon extract on low speed until creamed.
2. Scrape the sides of the bowl, then increase the speed to medium-low. Cream for another 3 minutes. Scrape the bowl again, then cream on high speed for 1 minute, until the frosting is thoroughly mixed.
3. Remove and place into a piping bag or an airtight container and refrigerate. (The frosting can made and stored in the refrigerator for up to 7 days. If using from the refrigerator, let the frosting sit at room temperature for 10 to 15 minutes before piping it.)

The Build

Pipe the frosting on the top of each cake and sprinkle citrus sugar on the frosting. Garnish each cake with blackberries and powdered sugar.

Spanish Hot Chocolate Cake

The Mayans and Incas created a chocolate drink that was considered to be an aphrodisiac. In addition to chocolate, it had cinnamon, rose water, saffron, chiles, and vanilla—ingredients that released "feel good" endorphins. I love telling that story to restaurant guests. Their expressions immediately shift to excitement, and it piques an interest that usually sells them on this dessert. In this cake, the sweetness of the orange cuts through the richness of the chocolate and rounds out the bitterness. I recommend eating a bite of the cake, then taking a bite of orange. It is delicious.

MAKES SIX (6-INCH) CAKES OR THREE (9-INCH) CAKES

FOR THE CAKE
Butter or pan spray, for greasing
3 cups self-rising flour
2 cups granulated sugar
1 tablespoon ground cinnamon
1 teaspoon xanthan gum
Pinch of saffron
½ teaspoon kosher salt
¼ teaspoon crushed red pepper
2 cups buttermilk
1½ cups freshly brewed coffee
¼ cup vegetable oil
2 large eggs
¼ cup sour cream
1 tablespoon vanilla bean paste or
    vanilla extract
1 teaspoon rose water, preferably Cortas
1 cup bittersweet chocolate chips

FOR THE GANACHE
1 cup heavy cream
1 tablespoon ground cinnamon
1 teaspoon vanilla extract
Pinch of saffron
Pinch of crushed red pepper
1 teaspoon rose water, preferably Cortas
2 cups bittersweet chocolate chips

FOR THE BUILD
¼ cup mini marshmallows
Powdered sugar, for dusting
Orange slices, for garnish

Make the Cake

1. Preheat the oven to 325°F. Grease your pans of choice.
2. Combine the flour, sugar, cinnamon, xanthan gum, saffron, salt, and crushed red pepper in a large bowl.
3. Add the buttermilk, coffee, oil, eggs, sour cream, vanilla bean paste, and rose water to the flour mixture and whisk thoroughly to combine. Fold in the chocolate chips.
4. Divide the batter among the cake pans and place the pans on a sheet pan.
5. Bake the cakes for 7 minutes. Rotate the sheet pan and bake for another 7 minutes, or until a toothpick inserted into the center of each cake comes out clean.
6. Let the cakes cool to room temperature. Once cool, remove the cakes from the pans. Place a serving plate/platter over a pan. Turn the plate over while holding the pan. Gently free the cake pan from the cake and place on a wire rack. Repeat for the remaining cakes.

Make the Ganache

1. Create a double boiler. Bring 2 inches of water to a simmer in a small saucepan. Place a stainless-steel or glass bowl on the saucepan (be sure the bottom doesn't touch the water).
2. Put the cream, cinnamon, vanilla, saffron, crushed red pepper, and rose water in the bowl and heat for 10 minutes, stirring occasionally, or until the cream mixture reaches 200°F on an instant-read thermometer.
3. Stir in the chocolate chips with a rubber spatula or wooden spoon until the chocolate is completely melted and thoroughly mixed with the cream, and the mixture has thickened. Remove from the heat. (The ganache can be made up to this point and stored in a heat-proof container in the refrigerator for up to 2 weeks. To reheat, microwave in 1-minute increments until soft. It can also be reheated in a double boiler.)

The Build

Spread the ganache on the cakes. Decorate the cakes with mini marshmallows. Use a kitchen torch to toast the marshmallows and gently melt the ganache. Dust with powdered sugar and garnish with orange slices.

Guava Duff Cake

I was introduced to guava duff when I was working in the Bahamas. Traditionally, it is presented like a jelly roll—guava paste rolled in white cake and topped with a warm coconut-guava sauce. Guava is a unique tropical fruit that grows in the Caribbean. It has a slightly tart and subtly sweet flavor. This version of the cake is baked in nine-inch cake pans and is perfect to serve on a beautiful spring day or cool summer night.

MAKES THREE (9-INCH) CAKES

FOR THE MACERATED PINEAPPLE
1 small pineapple, peeled, cored, and cut
    into medium dice (2 cups)
½ cup granulated sugar
¼ cup spiced rum
1 teaspoon vanilla bean paste or vanilla extract
1 teaspoon ground ginger
¼ bunch mint, leaves only, thinly sliced (½ cup)

FOR THE CAKE
Butter or pan spray, for greasing
1 cup guava paste
½ cup water
3 cups self-rising flour
1 cup granulated sugar
1 cup sweetened grated coconut
1 tablespoon ground ginger
1 teaspoon xanthan gum
½ teaspoon kosher salt
2 cups canned coconut milk
Juice of 7 or 8 limes (1 cup)
¼ cup refined coconut oil, melted
2 large eggs
¼ cup sour cream
1 tablespoon vanilla bean paste or
    vanilla extract

FOR THE FROSTING
14 ounces guava paste
1 cup (2 sticks) salted butter, softened
8 ounces vegetable shortening
1 (8-ounce) block cream cheese
8 ounces powdered sugar
¼ cup canned coconut milk

FOR THE BUILD
2 cups sweetened shredded coconut
Powdered sugar, for dusting

**Make the
Macerated Pineapple**

Put the pineapple, sugar, rum, vanilla, and ginger in a medium bowl and gently toss together. Fold in the mint just prior to serving. (The macerated pineapple can be made ahead, stored in an airtight container in the refrigerator, for up to 3 days.)

Make the Cake

1. Preheat the oven to 325°F. Grease the pans.
2. Put the guava paste and water in a small saucepan. Cook on low heat until the guava paste softens. Remove from the heat and puree the guava paste with a handheld stick blender until smooth.
3. Combine the flour, sugar, coconut, ginger, xanthan gum, and salt in a large bowl.
4. Whisk the guava puree into the flour mixture. Whisk the coconut milk, lime juice, coconut oil, eggs, sour cream, and vanilla bean paste into the guava-flour mixture.
5. Divide the batter among the cake pans and place the pans on a sheet pan.
6. Bake the cakes for 7 minutes. Rotate the cakes and bake for another 7 minutes, or until a toothpick inserted into the center of each cake comes out clean.
7. Let the cakes cool to room temperature. Once cool, remove the cakes from the pans. Place a serving plate/platter over a pan. Turn the plate over while holding the pan. Gently free the cake pan from the cake and place on a wire rack. Repeat for the remaining cakes.

Make the Frosting

1. In a microwave-safe bowl, microwave the guava paste for 2 minutes to soften. Cool to room temperature.
2. In the bowl of a stand mixer with the paddle attachment, mix the softened guava paste, butter, shortening, cream cheese, and powdered sugar on low speed for 3 minutes.
3. Scrape the sides of the bowl and add the coconut milk. Mix on low speed for 1 minute. Scrape the sides of the bowl. Increase the mixer speed to medium-low and mix for 2 minutes. Scrape the sides of the bowl one final time and mix on high speed for 1 minute.

The Build

1. Preheat the oven to 325°F. Spread the shredded coconut on a sheet pan and bake in the oven for 7 minutes, or until golden brown.
2. Pipe the frosting on the cakes. Sprinkle the toasted coconut on top of each cake, then dust with powdered sugar. Garnish with the macerated pineapple.

Della's Sweet Potato Pie

My uncle Leon came to visit us all the time when I was a kid. He was in the military, stationed at Fort Bragg. The first pie I ever made was with him. He was craving my grandmother's sweet potato pie, and we made it from scratch together. In Black culture, sweet potato pie is our traditional Thanksgiving pie. It is a dessert I crave during the holidays, but it is certainly great year-round.

MAKES TWO (9-INCH) PIES

INGREDIENTS

FOR THE SAUCE
1 cup buttermilk
2 cups powdered sugar
1 tablespoon vanilla bean paste or
    vanilla extract
Pinch of freshly cracked black pepper

FOR THE VANILLA WHIPPED CREAM
¾ cup heavy cream
¼ cup powdered sugar
¼ teaspoon vanilla bean paste or extract

FOR THE FILLING
3 pounds sweet potatoes, coarsely diced
    (6 cups)
1 cup condensed milk
2 cups evaporated milk
6 large eggs
1 cup packed light brown sugar
2 tablespoons ground cinnamon
1 tablespoon ground ginger
1 tablespoon ground cardamom
1 tablespoon vanilla bean paste or
    vanilla extract
1 teaspoon kosher salt

FOR THE PIE DOUGH
5 cups self-rising flour, plus more for dusting
½ cup (1 stick) salted butter, cut into pieces
½ cup vegetable shortening
½ cup granulated sugar
1 cup ice-cold water

FOR THE BUILD
Powdered sugar, for dusting
Fresh blackberries, for garnish

Make the Sauce

Puree the buttermilk, powdered sugar, vanilla extract, and pepper in a bowl with a handheld stick blender. Alternatively, whisk until smooth. (Store in an airtight container in the refrigerator until ready to serve. It can be made up to 7 days in advance.)

Make the Whipped Cream

Whisk the heavy cream and powdered sugar in a stainless-steel bowl until soft peaks form. Alternatively, use a hand mixer. Fold in the vanilla. Transfer to an airtight container and refrigerate until ready to serve.

Make the Pie Filling

1. Preheat the oven to 400°F. Wrap the sweet potatoes in foil and place on a sheet pan. Bake for 1½ hours, or until fork-tender. Let the sweet potatoes cool. Once cool enough to handle, remove the foil and peel them, discarding the skin.
2. Put the sweet potatoes, milks, eggs, brown sugar, cinnamon, ginger, cardamom, vanilla bean paste, and salt in a large bowl. Puree the mixture with a handheld stick blender until smooth. Set aside until ready to use.

Make the Pie Dough

1. In the bowl of a stand mixer with the paddle attachment, thoroughly mix the flour, butter, shortening, and sugar. With the mixer running, slowly pour in the ice-cold water.
2. Once the dough forms, transfer it to a clean work surface lightly dusted with flour. Dust the dough with flour, then knead until it comes together. Wrap the dough in plastic wrap and let it rest for 10 minutes.
3. Divide the dough in half and flatten each half into a disc. Add more flour to your work surface.
4. Use a rolling pin to roll out each dough disc to cover a 9-inch pie plate, or about ¹⁄₁₆ inch thick.
5. Gently lift the dough circles and fit them into the pie pans, lining the bottoms and sides. Pinch or crimp the edges with a fork, then prick the bottom with a fork.
6. Line both pie shells with parchment paper and fill with dried baking beans. Rest the pie shells for 15 minutes before baking. Preheat the oven to 325°F.
7. Bake the pie shells for 15 minutes in the oven. Remove from the oven and remove the parchment paper with baking beans. Reserve the pie shells until ready to fill.

Make the Pie

1. Divide the filling among the pie shells.
2. Place the pies on the center rack and bake for 20 minutes. Rotate the pans and bake for an additional 10 minutes, or until a toothpick inserted into the center of each pie comes out clean. Allow the pies to cool.

The Build

Spoon some of the sauce into the center of a plate. Slice the pie and place a piece on the sauce, and top with a spoonful of whipped cream. Dust the pie with powdered sugar and garnish with fresh blackberries. Plate the remaining servings.

Chocolate-Bourbon Pecan Pie

My parents always had fresh, unshelled mixed nuts out on the table along with a cracker. It was a snack I found in every household I entered growing up in Cleveland. Pecan pie is a traditional Southern dessert, but in Kentucky, they add chocolate and bourbon. The variety of spices in this dish, including Chinese five-spice powder, is what makes this pie unique. Fire-spice powder is a combination of cinnamon, star anise, fennel seed, Sichuan pepper, and cloves, creating a complex blend, which, combined with chocolate and bourbon, provides layers of flavor in each bite.

MAKES TWO (9-INCH) PIES

FOR THE PIE FILLING
1 cup (2 sticks) salted butter
1 cup packed light brown sugar
1½ cups cane syrup, preferably Alaga
1 cup honey
½ cup molasses
1 tablespoon Chinese five-spice powder
1 tablespoon ground cinnamon
1 tablespoon vanilla bean paste or vanilla
    extract
¼ cup bourbon
¼ cup self-rising flour
6 large eggs

FOR THE PIE DOUGH
5 cups self-rising flour, plus more for dusting
½ cup (1 stick) salted butter
½ cup vegetable shortening
½ cup granulated sugar
1 cup ice-cold water

FOR THE PIE
4 cups whole pecans
2 cups bittersweet chocolate chips

FOR THE BUILD
Powdered sugar, for dusting

Make the Filling

1. Put the butter and brown sugar in a medium saucepan and cook on medium heat, stirring, until the butter and sugar melt. Continue to stir and cook until the sugar caramelizes.
2. Add the cane syrup, honey, and molasses to the butter-sugar mixture and cook on medium-high heat for 10 minutes, stirring often.
3. Off the heat, add the Chinese five-spice powder, cinnamon, vanilla, bourbon, flour, and eggs. Puree the mixture with a handheld stick blender until smooth. Alternatively, whisk by hand.
4. Reserve until ready to use. (The filling can be stored in an airtight container in the refrigerator for up to 7 days.)

Make the Pie Dough

1. In the bowl of a stand mixer with the paddle attachment, thoroughly mix the flour, butter, shortening, and sugar. With the mixer running, slowly pour in the ice-cold water.
2. Once the dough forms, transfer it to a clean work surface lightly dusted with flour. Dust the dough with flour, then knead until it comes together. Wrap the dough in plastic wrap and let it rest for 10 minutes.
3. Divide the dough in half and flatten each half into a disc. Add more flour to your work surface.
4. Use a rolling pin to roll out each dough disc to cover a nine-inch pie plate, or about $\frac{1}{16}$ inch thick.
5. Gently lift the dough circles and fit them into the pie pans, lining the bottoms and sides. Pinch or crimp the edges with a fork, then prick the bottom with a fork.
6. Line both pie shells with parchment paper and fill with dried baking beans. Rest the pie shells for 15 minutes before baking. Preheat the oven to 325°F.
7. Bake the pie shells for 15 minutes. Remove from the oven and remove the parchment paper with baking beans. Reserve the pie shells until ready to fill.

Make the Pie

1. Place 2 cups of the pecans and 1 cup of the chocolate chips into each pie crust. Divide the filling between the pie shells.
2. Bake the pies for 20 minutes, then rotate and cook for another 15 minutes, or until a toothpick inserted into the center of each pie comes out clean. Allow the pies to cool.

The Build

Cut a wedge of pie and dust with powdered sugar. Plate the remaining servings.

Strawberry-Rosemary Cobbler Pie

Incorporating a savory into sweets is a technique I have used throughout my career as a chef. In this dessert, there is a complexity of flavor that really shines. The sweet strawberries and herbaceousness of the rosemary provide a brightness to this dish that complements the acidity and sweetness of the limoncello in the light, airy Chantilly cream. The hint of pepper brings a little heat and depth to the cream while adding another dimension of flavor. Together, when combined with the citrus cake batter, these ingredients create a spectacular pie that is light and delicious.

FOR THE PIE DOUGH
5 cups self-rising flour
½ cup (1 stick) salted butter
½ cup vegetable shortening
½ cup granulated sugar
1 cup ice-cold water

FOR THE FILLING
4 pints strawberries
1 cup granulated sugar
2 tablespoons chopped fresh rosemary
Juice of 1 lemon (2 tablespoons)
1 teaspoon xanthan gum
2 cups Florida Citrus Cake batter
   (see page 254)

FOR THE CHANTILLY CREAM
1 cup heavy cream
½ cup powdered sugar
¼ cup limoncello
¼ teaspoon freshly ground black pepper

FOR THE BUILD
1 cup halved fresh strawberries, for garnish
¼ cup powdered sugar, for dusting

Make the Pie Dough

1. In the bowl of a stand mixer with the paddle attachment, thoroughly mix the flour, butter, shortening, and sugar. With the mixer running, slowly pour in the ice-cold water.
2. Once the dough forms, transfer it to a clean work surface lightly dusted with flour. Dust the dough with flour, then knead until it comes together. Wrap the dough in plastic wrap and let it rest for 10 minutes.
3. Divide the dough in half and flatten each half into a disc. Add more flour to your work surface.
4. Use a rolling pin to roll out each dough disk to cover a nine-inch pie plate, or about $\frac{1}{16}$ inch thick.
5. Gently lift the dough circles and fit them into the pie pans, lining the bottoms and sides. Pinch or crimp the edges with a fork, then prick the bottom with a fork.
6. Line both pie shells with parchment paper and fill with dried baking beans. Rest the pie shells for 15 minutes before baking.
7. Bake the pie shells for 15 minutes. Remove from the oven and remove the parchment paper with baking beans. Reserve the pie shells until ready to fill.

Make the Filling and Pie

1. Gently mix the strawberries, sugar, rosemary, lemon juice, and xanthan gum in a medium bowl.
2. Fill each pie shell with 1 cup of the citrus cake batter. Divide the strawberry mixture evenly between the two pies.
3. Bake the pies for 24 minutes. Rotate and cook for another 15 minutes, or until a toothpick inserted into the center of each pie comes out clean. Allow the pies to cool.

Make the Chantilly

1. In the bowl of a stand mixer with the wire whip attachment, beat the heavy cream and sugar on low speed for 1 minute. Increase the speed to medium-low and mix until the cream starts to make peaks.
2. Add the limoncello and pepper and beat for 20 seconds to combine. Reserve until ready to serve.

The Build

Place a slice of pie in the center of a plate. Top with a dollop of Chantilly cream. Add a few fresh strawberries to the plate and dust with powdered sugar.

ACKNOWLEDGMENTS

This book would not have been possible without my mother and father, who instilled in me the discipline and passion to have faith in my voice. They gave me the mindset to challenge myself, and when I fall to always pick myself up and press forward. I would like to thank my wife, Anna, for believing in me from the start. She invested in my first restaurant, and she has been supportive in many ways through many projects. Our relationship has shaped me to become a better person.

I would like to thank all the chefs who have opened their kitchens to me throughout my career and the cooks I have worked with as well. I am so grateful to my good friend Chef Scott Schwartz, who provided me with an opportunity during one of the most humbling and challenging times in my career while navigating the Covid-19 pandemic. The hours we spent working together and swapping stories helped shape the concept of this cookbook. I truly cherish that time in the kitchen with you. A sincere thanks to Jennifer Booker, Matt and Ted Lee, Virginia Willis, Alexander Smalls, and Adrian Miller for your wisdom, time, and care in advising me and my team on this project. I am forever grateful and in your debt. Also thank you to Sonny Sweetman, my brother from another mother. Over the course of more than twenty years of friendship, you have made me a better person and stronger culinary professional.

To Nan Kavanaugh, my cowriter on this project, thank you for helping me bring my stories to life on the page. Since we met over a decade ago, you have been sharing the stories of my food. That connection has brought us to this project and the chance to create something bigger than ourselves. To Kristen Penoyer, your gift as a photographer is nothing but pure talent. Over the years we have worked together, you have created a canvas for my food beyond anything I could have imagined. Thank you to the recipe testers who gave their time and resources to supporting this project: my brother, Kirk Gilbert, Diane Baynes, Tory Eulenfeld, Nan and Eugene Gibson, Jeanne Loomis, Stephen Roberts, Cindy Sutton, Anna Vansickle, and George Veale. I would also like to thank the Strothman Agency and Rizzoli for believing in this project and giving us the opportunity to bring it to the world.

Finally, I would like to thank God for giving me the mental strength to continue this path through so many trials and tribulations. From becoming a young widower raising a baby girl to surviving cancer, thank you, God, for giving me the ability to be strong and keep going, because I understand that there is a higher purpose.

KENNY GILBERT

Chef Kenny Gilbert is best known for his appearance on *Top Chef* season seven, where he displayed a big personality and instantly became one of the most likable cheftestants to date. An award-winning chef and restaurateur, Gilbert's career spans over two decades and has graced him with opportunities to travel around the world and learn the authentic techniques and flavors of global cuisines. He has always had a love of cooking. He grew up in Cleveland, Ohio, with family roots in the South. His father was an avid BBQ man and his mother, a fantastic home cook.

Gilbert has been featured on a variety of national television programs and competitions: he won on *Beat Bobby Flay*, *Midnight Feast*, and *Cutthroat Kitchen*; he was a judge on *Chopped Junior*; and he has been on *CBS Saturday Morning, The Today Show,* as well as HGTV. His recipes have been published in a multitude of national magazines and blogs including *Food & Wine, Coastal Living, Garden & Gun, Men's Journal,* and *O Magazine*. Oprah Winfrey often taps Gilbert to cater festivities at her home as one of her preferred personal chefs. His dishes can be found in numerous cookbooks, such as Oprah Winfrey's *Food, Health, and Happiness: 115 On-Point Recipes for Great Meals and a Better Life,* Battman's *Toques in Black*, Adrian Miller's *Black Smoke*, Bobby Flay's *Beat Bobby Flay*, and *Art Culinaire*.

An entrepreneur, Gilbert launched a product line of spices and sauces in 2015. His restaurant, Silkie's Chicken & Champagne Bar, is in Jacksonville, Florida, and it showcases a global take on the iconic Southern chicken and biscuits.

NAN KAVANAUGH

An award-winning editor and writer, Nan Kavanaugh has worked in both the media and the restaurant industries for nearly two decades. Her writings on culture, food, health, and travel are rooted in her deep appreciation for authentic storytelling and human connection. An avid home cook and lover of great wine and good company, she lives in North Carolina with her husband Chef Scott Schwartz and their two daughters.

KRISTEN PENOYER

Kristen Penoyer is a professional photographer and self-professed "food nerd" with a passion for documenting the culinary world, from seed to plate. A serial creative, she boasts an impressive freelance career spanning twenty years. She has launched multiple businesses in the field of photography, working with boutique and national brands alike and bringing her seasoned eye and signature style to the table.

Of the 4,000-plus photos we took to make this cookbook, we originally selected a beautiful food shot for the cover. But when the team at Rizzoli suggested this image, it made so much more sense. This cover photograph resonates with essential themes that run through this cookbook: family, friendship, heritage, and diversity.

All things tell stories. My brother, Kirk, is both a talented chef and a ceramicist. He made the small pitcher and the black bowl on the butcher block. The Japanese Shun knife was a surprise gift from my childhood friend, Michael Dibaltolomeo. He had heard through the grapevine that I had lost a bunch of knives at an event, and out of the blue, he sent me this incredible tool. The apron is also a gift through the industry. It is made by BA Craftmade Aprons, a company owned by a mother in Minnesota whose business began with her making aprons for her three chef sons and grew through word of mouth. The dish holding the bulgogi (a recipe I learned from my best friend, Rey Eugenio, who is Filipino), along with entire sets of Steelite dishware, were donated for this photo shoot by another wonderful friend in the industry, Kim Matienzo, VP of Global Marketing for Steelite. The objects in this photo tell an amazing story about friendship and generosity, and connect with the idea that kitchens are places of storytelling.

The quilt blocks on the wall have a story that is truly special to me. When I opened Gilbert's Underground Kitchen on Amelia Island, in Florida, my friend Rey and his wife gifted me the two blocks. They are talking quilt patterns from the Underground Railroad, used to communicate with enslaved people as they traveled the road to freedom. The block with the square in the middle is known as the "Monkey Wrench" pattern, which signaled to enslaved people that they needed to prepare themselves with the physical, mental, and spiritual tools necessary for a long journey. The other block is the "Crossroads" pattern, which meant safe passage to freedom, specifically to Cleveland, Ohio, which was an important destination and hub of the Underground Railroad. I grew up in the suburbs of Cleveland. Underground Kitchen was the first restaurant I opened on my own, and these quilt blocks continue to be a powerful reminder of my history as an American, as well as of the journey of my life. The support of my family, friends, and colleagues has helped me so much as a chef, bringing me to this place, and for that I am incredibly grateful.

First published in the United States of America in 2023 by
Rizzoli International Publications, Inc.
300 Park Avenue South
New York, NY 10010
www.rizzoliusa.com

Photographer: Kristen Penoyer

Publisher: Charles Miers
Associate Publisher: James Muschett
Editor: Tricia Levi
Designer: Susi Oberhelman
Production Manager: Colin Hough Trapp
Managing Editor: Lynn Scrabis

Printed in China

2023 2024 2025 2026 / 10 9 8 7 6 5 4 3 2 1

ISBN: 978-0-8478-9925-8

Library of Congress Control Number: 2022947079

Visit us online:
Facebook.com/RizzoliNewYork
Twitter: @Rizzoli_Books
Instagram.com/RizzoliBooks
Pinterest.com/RizzoliBooks
Youtube.com/user/RizzoliNY
Issuu.com/Rizzoli